The Good Person of Sichuan

The gods come to earth to search for a thoroughly good person and find the penniless prostitute Shen Te. But when greedy neighbours take advantage of her good nature, she is forced to adopt the persona of a fictitious male cousin, Shui Ta.

This famous parable was written on the eve of the Second World War and is translated here by Michael Hofmann.

The Good Person of Sichuan was staged at the National Theatre in November 1989 in a production directed by Deborah Warner and starring Fiona Shaw.

Bertolt Brecht was born in Augsburg on 10 February, 1898, and died in Berlin on 14 August, 1956. He grew to maturity as a playwright in the frenetic years of the twenties and early thirties, with such plays as *Man Equals Man*, *The Threepenny Opera*, *Mahagonny* and *The Mother*. He left Germany when Hitler came to power in 1933, eventually reaching the United States in 1941, where he remained until 1947. It was during this period of exile that such masterpieces as *The Life of Galileo*, *Mother Courage* and *The Caucasian Chalk Circle* were written. Shortly after his return to Europe in 1947 he founded the Berliner Ensemble, and from then until his death was mainly occupied in producing his own plays.

Michael Hofmann was born in Freiburg in 1957, educated at Cambridge, and lives in London. He has published two books of poems with Faber and Faber, *Nights in the Iron Hotel* (1983) and *Acrimony* (1986), and has translated books by Beat Sterchi, Joseph Roth and Wim Wenders.

BERTOLT BRECHT

The Good Person of Sichuan

a parable play

(A version made for the National Theatre,
based on the Santa Monica version, 1943)

translated by
Michael Hofmann

METHUEN DRAMA

A METHUEN MODERN PLAY

First published in this translation in Great Britain in 1989 by
Methuen Drama, Michelin House, 81 Fulham Road, London SW3 6RB,
by arrangement with Suhrkamp Verlag, Frankfurt am Main.

Translation copyright © 1989 Stefan S. Brecht
Translator's Preface © 1989 Methuen Drama

Original work entitled
Der gute Mensch von Setzuan
Copyright 1955 by Suhrkamp Verlag, Berlin

A CIP catalogue record for this book is available from the
British Library.

ISBN 0-413-63550-3

The front cover is from the National Theatre poster:
painting by Bruce McLean, designed by Michael Mayhew.
The photograph on the back cover is by Gerda Goedhart.

Printed and bound in Great Britain by Cox & Wyman Ltd, Reading

Translator's Preface

This translation was commissioned by Deborah Warner for her production of the play at the National Theatre in 1989-90. The text she wanted to use is basically the 'Santa Monica version' of 1943, worked up by Brecht and his collaborators from the 1941 'Zurich' original with a view to American production. The 'Santa Monica' version is shorter and faster; it cuts out characters, scenes and whole elements of plot. In particular, it does away with the dippy financial complications of the original: the leases and rents, the loans and blank cheques made out for 10,000 dollars. It also sharpens the moral issues of the play by substituting opium for tobacco. It is surprising that this version of the play achieved no greater currency, but then there were no authorised productions of *The Good Person* – in either version – in Brecht's lifetime. Recently, though, there have been stagings of the 'Santa Monica' in both Germanies, and its inclusion (unfortunately, just too late for my purposes: I had to work from blotchy, atmospheric photo-copies) in the new 30-volume edition of Brecht from Aufbau/Suhrkamp should allow more readers and directors a choice.*

We didn't choose. We had our cake and ate it. We took the slimline text and beefed it up. The wedding-scene was reinstated: its loss was too painful to contemplate – and it would have meant the second half of the play being little more than the finale. Also three of the Interludes were taken in for rhythm and balance; otherwise the gods would have disappeared from the middle of the play altogether. A very few lines have been tampered with for the sake of consistency. I hope our resulting text combines the purposefulness and drive of 'Santa Monica' with the egregious beauties of 'Zurich'.

*

In the popular estimation, Brecht is thought of as a colloquial playwright but this really isn't the case. He can be colloquial, he

---

*The 'Santa Monica version' was first published in English by Methuen London in 1985 as a series of notes to the Brecht Collected Plays, Vol.6i, *The Good Person of Szechwan*, translated by John Willet, edited by John Willett and Ralph Manheim often is, but there is no register that he cannot – and will not – use. Formally, *The Good Person of Sichuan* contains everything: rhymed songs, blank verse, free verse, Chinese proverbs and poems. A notorious stage-direction begins 'In a great speech, Shen Te . . .' Brecht is a rhetorician, a formidable organiser of material. The ensemble scenes in the shop and the restaurant are master-pieces of surprise, logic and timing. Scene Three, 'The City Park in the Evening' is almost unbearably touching, but it is itself unmoved: there are no tears in its eyes. So, style and tone are variables in Brecht: the fixed points are economy and force. The scene and the argument take precedence over the characters; an individual's way of speaking has no way of asserting itself against the conception of a scene. It is not a watercolourist's way of writing, but a physicist's.

Brecht has no interest in giving the illusion of naturalness. 'What' interests him; 'How' leaves him cold. He isn't bothered about making his water-seller speak 'just like a water-seller' – whatever that might be. What concerns him is that he should be able to go to the heart of his own – socio-economic – predicament. All his characters speak cleanly from this core of their being, rather than producing shallow, turbid scoops of consciousness from their edges. They say things that fit no 'character' because they are not confined within cultural, linguistic horizons. They speak with a deliberate inappropriateness, which, in English, may very easily be taken for parody or affectation, but which is nothing of the kind: it is the sum of their dramatic predicament, the uncommon intelligence with which they are endowed by their maker Brecht, and an almost anarchic pleasure in language.

*

These things – gestures towards 'epic theatre', the 'V'- or 'a'- word, and 'Brecht' – I have learned empirically from working on *The Good Person of Sichuan*. They confounded me as a translator, probably because an organic language is easier: image-complexes, leitmotivs, running gags, the timbre of a particular character. Brecht gives one nothing regular, nothing unthinking to 'slip into'. As he says in another context (*Of Poor B.B.*) 'Here you have someone on whom you can't rely': not a sentiment the translator should be heard to echo. Also, amazingly, I've had to battle to keep things short. Amazingly, because a German text will normally shrink by 15%, even 20% in English. Brecht, though, is so pared-down, so abrupt, that I've had to guard against putting in the little suave, consensual, smoothing-over phrases that English is so in love with. I only hope my Brecht is no longer than he is in German.

*

A translation for the stage – and this is the first I have done – must be in some measure a joint enterprise. I should like to thank Deborah Warner and the National's Nick Drake for their continuing scrutiny during production – a phase which, in book publication, is quiet as the grave – and the composer Dominic Muldowney and members of the cast for their suggestions and demurrals. I should also like to thank my father, the German writer Gert Hofmann, for showing me just how often Brecht can be strange, unaccountable and opaque.

Michael Hofmann
November 1989
London

'For the practice of virtue, a modicum of comfort is necessary.'

Thomas Aquinas

The Good Person of Sichuan opened at the National Theatre on 28 November 1989, with the following cast, in order of appearance:

WANG, *a water-seller*	Bill Paterson
FIRST GOD	Graham Valentine
SECOND GOD	Edward Harbour
THIRD GOD	Jeffrey Segal
SHEN TE	Fiona Shaw
MRS SHIN, *a widow*	Susan Engel
THE WIFE	Susan Colverd
THE HUSBAND	Bill Stewart
THE NEPHEW	David Schneider
THE UNEMPLOYED MAN	Albie Woodington
LIN TO, *a carpenter*	Richard Bremmer
THE BROTHER	Colin Hurley
THE SISTER-IN-LAW	Alison Peebles
THE GRANDFATHER	Charles Simon
THE BOY	Simon Gregor
THE NIECE	Sandy McDade
THE POLICEMAN	Stuart McGugan
YANG SUN, *an unemployed airman*	Pete Postlethwaite
MRS MI TZU, *a tobacco merchant*	Janet Henfrey
SHU FU, *a barber*	Oscar Quitak
MRS YANG, *Sun's mother*	Maria Charles
NI TZU, *a child*	Speedy Choo
CITIZEN OF SICHUAN	Nicola Slade

OLD PROSTITUTE, WAITER, PRIEST, PASSERS-BY in the Prologue and the Opium Den played by members of the Company.

Director Deborah Warner
Designer Sue Blane
Music Dominic Muldowney
Lighting Jean Kalman

Scene:
The city of Sichuan, which is half-westernized.

Prelude

A Street in the Capital of Sichuan Province

Evening. WANG, *the water-seller, introduces himself to the audience.*

WANG. I am a water-seller here in the capital of Sichuan province. Business is patchy. When water is scarce, I have to go miles for it. When it's plentiful I don't make any money. This whole province is impoverished. They say things are so bad that only the gods can help us now. So imagine my delight when I learn from a cattle dealer who gets around a lot, that some very senior gods have set out on a fact-finding mission, and may shortly be expected in Sichuan. Heaven is said to be perturbed by the many complaints that are coming its way. For three days now I've been keeping a lookout for them, here at the edge of the city, particularly around nightfall, in the hope that I may be the first to welcome them. I probably wouldn't get a look in later, they'll be surrounded by dignitaries, and generally mobbed. I only hope I can recognise them! They may not all arrive together. It's possible they'll turn up one by one to attract less attention. That can't be them over there, they're just coming off work. (*He looks at some workers passing by.*) Their shoulders are bowed from carrying loads all day. And that fellow can't possibly be a god, he's got inky fingers. I'd say he was an office worker at the cement factory. Even those two fine gentlemen (*Two gentlemen pass.*) don't look like gods to me, they have cruel faces, like people who dish out a lot of beatings, which gods don't need to do. But what about those three! Now we're in business! They're well-nourished, bear no trace of any occupation, and they have dust on their shoes – they must have come from afar. It's them! At your service, O Enlightened Ones!

He throws himself to the ground.

FIRST GOD (*chuffed*). Are we expected here then?

WANG (*giving them all drinks*). You have been for a long time. But only I was sure that you were coming.

FIRST GOD. We require a room for the night. Do you know of one?

WANG. One room? Innumerable rooms! The city is at your feet, oh Enlightened Ones: choose your address!

The gods exchange meaningful looks.

FIRST GOD. The nearest house will do, my son! Try the nearest house first!

WANG. It's just that I'm afraid of incurring the enmity of powerful people, if I happen to favour one of their number. You see, not many people can be useful to the likes of us, but almost anyone is able to do us harm.

FIRST GOD. We can make it an order then: Take the nearest house!

WANG. That'd be Mr Fo's over there! If you'll just be patient for a moment!

He runs across to a house and knocks on the door. It's opened, but one can see him being turned away. He returns a little hesitantly.

How annoying. Mr Fo happens not to be at home, and his servants daren't do anything without his permission, because he is terribly strict. He will be livid when he learns who has been turned away from his door.

THE GODS (*smiling*). Absolutely.

WANG. A moment longer please! The house next door belongs to the widow Su. She will be beside herself with joy.

He runs there, but is evidently turned away from there as well.

I'm just going to ask across the way now. She says she has only one small room which is not ready. I can well understand her embarrassment at having some of the corners of her house less than clean. Women are like that, it's too bad. I'll go to Mr Cheng.

SECOND GOD. But a small room's quite sufficient. Tell her we'll take it.

WANG. But if it's untidy? It may be crawling with spiders.

SECOND GOD. Never mind that. Many spiders, fewer flies.

THIRD GOD. I say. (*Amiably to* WANG.) Go to Mr Cheng or whomever, my son. I must confess I am a little afraid of spiders.

WANG *knocks somewhere else and is admitted.*

VOICE FROM WITHIN THE HOUSE. Leave us alone with your gods! We've got other worries!

WANG (*returns to the gods*). Mr Cheng is inconsolable. He has a house full of relations, and is too scared to tell you so himself. Between you and me, I suspect there are some bad people among them, whom he doesn't want you to see. He's afraid of your judgement, that's the truth of it.

THIRD GOD. Are we really so terrible?

WANG. Only to bad people, isn't that right? In Kwan province, for instance, they've suffered flooding for decades now.

SECOND GOD. Oh? And why is that?

WANG. Well, because people there lack piety!

SECOND GOD. Nonsense. It's because they let the dam fall into disrepair!

FIRST GOD. Psst! (*To* WANG.) My son, are you at all optimistic?

WANG. What a question! I need only knock on the very next door, and I can have the pick of all the rooms in the house for you. People are desperate to put you up! A few regrettable mischances, you understand! Here I go!

He goes, hesitantly, and stops in the street, undecided.

SECOND GOD. What did I tell you?

THIRD GOD. It might still just be bad luck.

SECOND GOD. Bad luck in Shun, bad luck in Kwan, now bad luck in Sichuan! There is no more piety, that's the truth of the matter, and you won't admit it. Our mission is a failure.

FIRST GOD. But we may find good people at any moment. We

mustn't give up too easily.

THIRD GOD. The terms of the resolution were that the world can stay the way it is, if enough good people can be found who are able to lead a decent life. Unless I am very much mistaken, the water-seller himself is an example of such a man.

He goes across to WANG, *who is still standing there, undecided.*

SECOND GOD. He's very much mistaken. When the water man gave us all a drink from his cup, I noticed something. Look at it.

He shows it to the FIRST GOD.

FIRST GOD. It has a false bottom!

SECOND GOD. He's a cheat.

FIRST GOD. All right, cross him off then. But what does it matter if one apple is slightly rotten! We'll find plenty of people who come up to our requirements. We've got to find one! For two thousand years now there's been this chorus: the world can't go on as it is! No one can remain virtuous. – We must finally come up with some individuals who are in a position to observe our commandments.

THIRD GOD (*to* WANG). Is it too difficult to find lodgings?

WANG. For you! Certainly not! I ought to have come up with something right away. The blame is entirely mine for looking badly.

THIRD GOD. It certainly isn't that.

He goes back.

WANG. They're beginning to notice. (*He addresses a* GENTLEMAN.) Excuse me for venturing to address you, sir, but three of the highest gods, whose promised visit has been the talk of Sichuan for years, have just arrived and are seeking lodgings. Don't pass on: see for yourself! You can tell at a glance! For God's sake, seize the opportunity! Chance of a lifetime! Be the first on your block to ask the gods to stay, before someone else snaps them up, they will accept any serious offer.

THE GENTLEMAN *has passed on.*

(*Turning to another.*) Sir, you heard what this is about. Do you have a spare room? It needn't be palatial. It's the thought that counts.

THE GENTLEMAN. How do I know who these gods of yours are? There's no knowing who you'll end up giving a bed to.

He goes into a tobacconist's shop. WANG *hurries back to the trio.*

WANG. I've found a gentleman who's certain to say yes.

He sees his cup on the ground, looks in confusion at the gods, picks it up and runs back.

FIRST GOD. That doesn't sound too encouraging.

WANG (*when the* GENTLEMAN *comes out of the shop*). So what about offering them hospitality, then?

THE GENTLEMAN. How do you know I'm not staying at a hotel myself?

FIRST GOD. He won't find anything. We'll have to cross Sichuan off as well.

WANG. They are three of the principal gods! Honestly: I tell you, their statuettes in the temple are a very good likeness. If you hurry over and ask them, they may still accept.

THE GENTLEMAN (*laughs*). Who are these gangsters you're trying to palm off on everybody. (*Exit.*)

WANG (*calling after him*). Where's your faith, you miserable louse! You'll boil in brimstone for your lack of charity! The gods shit on you! Your grandchildren's grandchildren will be paying for this! You've put the whole of Sichuan to shame! (*Pause.*) Now there's only the prostitute Shen Te left, and she can't say 'no'.

He calls: 'Shen Te'. She puts her head out of the upstairs window.

They've come, and I can't find accommodation for them. Will you put them up for the night?

SHEN TE. I'm afraid I can't, Wang. I'm expecting a client. How is it that you're unable to find anywhere for them?

WANG. I can't tell you now. This Sichuan is a real hole.

SHEN TE. I would have to not answer if he comes. Then he

might go away again. He wants to take me out somewhere.

WANG. Couldn't we come up now?

SHEN TE. But you'd have to keep your voices down. Can I be open with them?

WANG. No! They mustn't learn of your occupation! We'd better wait on the street. Will you promise not to go off with your client?

SHEN TE. I haven't any money, and I'll be thrown out tomorrow morning unless I can pay my rent.

WANG. How can you even think of calculating at such a time?

SHEN TE. I don't know, the stomach rumbles even on the Emperor's birthday. But very well – I'll take them in.

She is seen turning the light down.

FIRST GOD. I'm afraid it's hopeless.

They go to WANG.

WANG (*gets a shock when he sees them standing behind him*). I've just found your accommodation.

He wipes his brow.

THE GODS. Really? Well let's go and see it then.

WANG. There's really no hurry. Take your time. The room is still being got ready.

THIRD GOD. Well then, let's sit down here and wait.

WANG. Isn't it a bit busy here? I suggest we go over there.

SHEN TE. We like observing people. It's what we came to do.

WANG. Isn't it a bit draughty here?

SHEN TE. Oh, we're hardy folk.

WANG. What would you say to a tour of Sichuan by night? I'll take you for a little stroll.

THIRD GOD. Actually we've done quite a lot of walking today already. (*Smiles.*) But if you want us out of the way, why don't you just say so?

They go back.

THIRD GOD. What about here?

They sit down on some steps, WANG on the ground a little to one side.

WANG (*with a rush*). Look, the accommodation I've found you is with a young unmarried woman. She's the best person in Sichuan.

THIRD GOD. That's nice.

WANG (*to the audience*). When I went to pick up my cup just now, they looked at me in a peculiar way. Do you suppose they noticed anything? I hardly dare look them in the eye any more.

THIRD GOD. You look quite exhausted.

WANG. Yes, it's all that running around.

FIRST GOD. Is life a struggle for people here?

WANG. It is for the good ones anyway.

FIRST GOD (*penetratingly*). And for you?

WANG. I take your meaning. I'm not good. But it's not easy for me either.

In the meantime a gentleman has appeared in front of SHEN TE's house, and whistled several times. On each occasion WANG flinches.

THIRD GOD (*quietly to WANG*). I think he's gone now.

WANG (*flummoxed*). Oh, all right.

He gets up and runs to the square, leaving behind his gear. But in the meantime, the following has happened: the waiting man has gone away, and SHEN TE, stepping outside her door, and quietly calling: 'Wang' has gone off down the street, looking for him. So when WANG now quietly calls: 'Shen Te', there is no answer.

She's given me the slip. She's gone off to make her rent, and I have no lodgings for the Enlightened Ones. They're tired and tired of waiting. I can't possibly go back to them again and say: Sorry, it's off! My own place in the sewage pipe is out of the question. Besides, these gods certainly wouldn't care to stay with a person whose shabby tricks they've seen through. I'm not going back to them, nothing will induce me to. But my gear is with them. What shall I do? I don't dare go and pick it up. I'm going to leave Sichuan and hide away somewhere, since I've failed to do a service to those I worship.

He hurtles off. No sooner has he gone, than SHEN TE *returns, looking on the other side, where she sees the gods.*

SHEN TE. Are you the Enlightened Ones? I am Shen Te. I would be happy if you agreed to come and stay in my little room.

THIRD GOD. Where did the water-seller go?

SHEN TE. I must have just missed him.

FIRST GOD. He must have thought you weren't coming, and felt too afraid to face us again.

THIRD GOD (*picks up the gear*). We'll leave this with you. He'll be wanting it later.

They go into the house, SHEN TE *leading the way. It gets dark, then light again. At dawn, the gods step outside the door, led by* SHEN TE, *who lights their way with a lamp. They take their leave.*

FIRST GOD. My dear Shen Te, we thank you for your hospitality. We shan't forget that it was you who took us in. Give the water-seller's gear back to him, and tell him we're grateful to him for showing us a good person.

SHEN TE. I am not good. I must confess: when Wang asked me to put you up, I hesitated.

FIRST GOD. It doesn't matter if you hesitate, so long as you make the correct decision. Let me tell you that you have given us more than a room for the night. There were many, even some of us gods, who doubted whether there were any good people left. It's largely to determine this that we have undertaken our journey. We continue on it now, joyful in the knowledge of having found such a person. Goodbye!

SHEN TE. Stay, Enlightened Ones, I am far from sure that I am good. I should like to be, but how do I make ends meet? Let me admit to you: I sell my body, but even then it's difficult, because there are so many who are driven to do the same. I am prepared to do anything, but who isn't? I would be only too happy to keep the commandments, to honour my mother and my father and to speak the truth. Not to covet my neighbour's house would be a joy to me, and to keep myself for one man would be pleasant. I too should like not to exploit my fellows, and not to rob the helpless. But how can I do all these things? Even breaking a few of the commandments, I have trouble enough.

FIRST GOD. All these, Shen Te, are nothing but the doubts of every good person.

THIRD GOD. Farewell, Shen Te! Send my regards to the water-seller! He was a good friend to us.

SECOND GOD. I'm afraid it's done little for him.

THIRD GOD. All the best!

FIRST GOD. Above all, be good, Shen Te. Farewell!

They turn to leave. Already they're waving goodbye.

SHEN TE (*afraid*). But I'm not sure of myself, O Enlightened Ones! How can I be good when everything is so expensive?

SECOND GOD. I'm afraid we can't help you there. We can't get involved in questions of economics.

THIRD GOD. Stop! Wait a minute! If she had a little more money, it might help her to be good.

SECOND GOD. We're not allowed to give her anything. We couldn't account for that up there.

FIRST GOD. Why not?

They put their heads together and hold an animated discussion.

(*To* SHEN TE, *in some embarrassment.*) We're told you can't raise the money to pay for your rent. We're not exactly poor, and so of course we'd like to pay for our accommodation. Here! (*He gives her some money.*) But don't tell anyone that we paid you. It might be misinterpreted.

SECOND GOD. Exactly.

THIRD GOD. No, we're within our rights. It's quite permissible to pay for your lodgings. There's nothing in the guidelines against it. Goodbye now!

The gods exeunt briskly.

Scene One

A Small Tobacco Shop

The shop is not yet fitted out completely, and is not yet open.

SHEN TE (*to the audience*). It's three days now since the gods went away. They told me they wanted to pay for their lodging and when I looked at what they had given me, I saw that it was more than a thousand silver dollars. With the money I bought myself this tobacco shop. I moved in here yesterday and hope to be able to do a great deal of good. For example, there is Mrs Shin, the former owner of the shop. Yesterday she came by for some rice for her children and today I see her coming across the square with her bowl.

Enter MRS SHIN. *The women bow to one another.*

SHEN TE. Good day, Mrs Shin.

MRS SHIN. Good day, Miss Shen Te. How do you like your new home?

SHEN TE. Very much. How did your children pass the night?

MRS SHIN. Oh, in a strange house, if you can call that hovel a house . . . The little one's coughing already.

SHEN TE. That's terrible.

MRS SHIN. Terrible. You've got no idea. You're doing very nicely, thank you. But running this dump will teach you a thing or two before you're through. It's a real slum out there!

SHEN TE. But you told me that the workers from the cement factory come in at lunchtime?

MRS SHIN. Yes, but they're the only ones who can afford to buy anything. Don't think you'll get any locals in here.

SHEN TE. You didn't tell me that when you sold me the shop.

MRS SHIN. Don't you start accusing me too. First of all you steal our home from us, and now you start calling it a dump and a slum! You've got some cheek. (*Cries.*)

SHEN TE (*quickly*). I'll get your rice.

MRS SHIN. I wanted to borrow some money off you as well.

SHEN TE (*while she pours rice into a bowl*). I can't lend you any. I haven't sold anything yet.

MRS SHIN. But I need it. What am I going to live on? You've taken everything off me. And now you're putting the screws on. I'll leave my children on your doorstep, you murderess!

She tears the pot of rice out of her hands.

SHEN TE. Don't get so cross! You'll only spill the rice!

Enter THE HUSBAND, THE WIFE *and* THE NEPHEW. THE WIFE *and* THE NEPHEW *are carrying sacks over their shoulders.*

THE WIFE. My dear Shen Te, we heard your fortunes have improved. You've become a businesswoman! But just think, we've lost our home! Our tobacco shop went broke. We wondered if we could take shelter here for the night, and put these two sacks in storage. Have you met my nephew? He's come along too, he goes everywhere with us.

THE NEPHEW (*looking round*). Nice shop you got here.

MRS SHIN. Who on earth are they?

SHEN TE. When I first came to the city from the country, they were my landlords. (*To the audience.*) When my bit of money was gone, they put me out on the street. They're probably afraid I may turn them away now.
They are poor.
They are homeless.
They are friendless.
They need someone.
– Who could turn them away?

Warmly, to the new arrivals.

Welcome! I'll gladly put you up. All I have though is this little room at the back of the shop.

THE HUSBAND. That'll do for us, don't worry.

THE WIFE (*while* SHEN TE *brings in tea*). The best thing is if we just settle down here at the back, so we don't get under your feet. Did you choose a tobacco shop because it reminded you of your first home? We'll be able to give you a few tips. That's another reason why we decided to come to you.

MRS SHIN (*ironically*). Let's hope a few customers come as well!

THE WIFE. Is that a dig at us?

THE HUSBAND. Psst! Here's a customer.

Enter THE UNEMPLOYED MAN.

THE UNEMPLOYED MAN. Excuse me, I'm out of work.

MRS SHIN *laughs.*

SHEN TE. How can I help?

THE UNEMPLOYED MAN. I hear you're opening your shop tomorrow. I thought you sometimes get breakages during transport. You wouldn't have a spare cigarette anywhere would you?

THE WIFE. He's got a nerve, asking for tobacco! It's not as though it was bread!

THE UNEMPLOYED MAN. Bread's more expensive. A couple of puffs at a cigarette, and I'll feel like a new man. I'm so knackered.

SHEN TE (*gives him cigarettes*). It's important to feel like a new man. I'll open my shop with you. You'll be my first customer, and bring me luck.

THE UNEMPLOYED MAN *quickly lights up, inhales and exits, coughing.*

THE WIFE. Was that right, dear Shen Te?

MRS SHIN. If that's the way you open the shop, you'll be out of business in three days.

THE HUSBAND. I'll bet he had some funds on him.

SHEN TE. He said he had nothing.

THE NEPHEW. How do you know he wasn't lying?

SHEN TE (*in anger*). How do I know he was?

THE WIFE (*shaking her head*). She just can't say no! You're too good, Shen Te. If you want to hold on to your shop, you'll have to learn to refuse people now and then.

THE HUSBAND. Just say the shop isn't yours. Say it belongs to some relative, who you're strictly accountable to, a cousin or something, couldn't you do that?

MRS SHIN. One could, if one weren't continually playing the benefactress.

SHEN TE (*laughs*). That's right! Next I'll turf you out, and then I'll have my rice back from you!

THE WIFE (*shocked*). Is that rice yours too?

SHEN TE (*to the audience*).
They are bad people.
They are no one's friends.
They begrudge others a bowl of rice.
They need everything for themselves.
– Who could blame them?

Enter THE CARPENTER, [LIN TO].

MRS SHIN (*sees him and gets up to go*). I'll look in again tomorrow then, shall I. (*Exit.*)

THE CARPENTER (*calls after her*). Mrs Shin, stop! I want a word with you!

THE WIFE. Is she a regular here then? Does she have any claim on you?

SHEN TE. No, she has no claim, but she's hungry.

THE CARPENTER. She'll know why she ran off like that. Are you the new owner of the shop? Ah, I see you're stocking the shelves. Did you know that they're not your shelves? Not unless you pay for them. The baggage who was sitting there never paid me for them. (*To the others.*) You see, I'm the carpenter.

SHEN TE. But I thought everything was included in the outfitting which I paid for.

THE CARPENTER. A swindle! Swindle! I bet you and that Mrs Shin are in this together. I want my fifty silver dollars, or my name's not Lin To.

SHEN TE. How can I pay, I haven't any money!

THE CARPENTER. Then I'll serve a distraining order on you. Right now! Pay up or I'll have you distrained!

THE HUSBAND (*whispers to* SHEN TE). Cousin!

SHEN TE. Couldn't you wait till next month?

THE CARPENTER (*shouting*). No!

SHEN TE. Don't be so unyielding, Mr Lin To. I can't meet all demands at once.

To the audience.
Clemency, a little forebearance and your forces are
   replenished.
Look at the carthorse stopping by a tuft of grass:
Turn a blind eye, and he'll pull better.
A little patience in June, and the tree
Will be weighed down by peaches come August. How,
Without patience, can we live together?
A short adjournment when you set off,
And the remotest destinations come within reach.

To THE CARPENTER.
Just be a little patient with me, Mr Lin To!

THE CARPENTER. And who's going to be patient with me and my family? (*He moves shelving away from the wall, as though to remove it.*) Pay up, or I'm taking my shelves away with me!

THE WIFE. My dear Shen Te, why don't you let your cousin take care of the matter? (*To* THE CARPENTER.) Write out an invoice, and Miss Shen Te's cousin will pay you.

THE CARPENTER. I've come across cousins like that before!

THE NEPHEW. What's so funny? I know him personally.

THE HUSBAND. Razor sharp.

THE CARPENTER. Very well, I'll write him a bill!

He turns the shelving upside down, sits down on it and writes out a bill.

THE WIFE (*to* SHEN TE). He'll have the shirt off your back for those few boards unless someone tells him where to get off. Don't ever accept a demand, whether justified or not, because you'll be inundated with demands, justified *and* not. Drop a piece of gristle in your rubbish, and all the butchers' dogs in the neighbourhood will be in your yard fighting for it. What are the courts for?

SHEN TE. The courts won't feed him if his labour doesn't. He has done his work and doesn't want to go away empty-handed. He has a family. It's bad that I'm not able to pay him! What will the gods say?

THE HUSBAND. You did your bit when you took us in, that was already more than generous.

Enter a limping man and a pregnant woman.

THE BROTHER (*to the couple*). So this is where you've got to! Some relatives you are, just leaving us on the corner without a word!

THE WIFE (*to* SHEN TE, *in embarrassment*). This is my brother Wung and my sister-in-law. (*To the two of them.*) Now please pipe down and sit quietly in the corner so you don't bother our old friend, Miss Shen Te. You can stay here, it's all right with her. (*To* SHEN TE.) I think we'd better make room for the two of them, my sister-in-law's in her fifth month. Or don't you think so?

SHEN TE. Yes. Welcome.

THE WIFE. Say thank you. Cups are at the back. (*To* SHEN TE.) They would have had no idea where to go. Just as well you've got this shop . . .

SHEN TE (*laughing to the audience, bringing tea*). Yes, just as well!

THE CARPENTER (*grumpily*). Here's the bill. (*Hands it over.*) I'll be back for the money in the morning. (*Exit.*)

THE NEPHEW (*calling after him boisterously*). Rest assured, cousin will pay!

THE SISTER-IN-LAW (*quietly to* THE NEPHEW). This here isn't going to last very long!

Enter THE BOY, *leading an old man* [THE GRANDFATHER].

THE BOY (*facing back*). There they are.

THE WIFE. Hello, grandfather. (*To* SHEN TE.) The good old man! He must have been worried about us. And hasn't the boy grown? He eats like a termite. Who else have you got with you?

THE HUSBAND (*looking outside*). Only your niece.

THE SISTER-IN-LAW (*quietly to* THE NEPHEW, *as a little girl* [THE NIECE] *comes in*). The rats are boarding the sinking ship!

THE WIFE (*to* SHEN TE). A young relative from the country. I hope we're not too many for you. There weren't so many of us when you were living with us, were there? Yes, we've become more numerous. The worse off we were, the more numerous we became. And the more numerous we became, the worse off we were.

But now we'll call a halt in here, otherwise we'll never get any peace. (*She bolts the door and all sit down.*) The main thing is that we don't get in the way of your running the business. Because what else is going to send smoke up the chimney? We planned something like this: the younger ones will go out during the day, and only grandfather, my sister-in-law and maybe myself will stay in. The rest can just look in now and again. Light the lamp over there and make yourselves at home.

THE NEPHEW (*humorously*). So long as the cousin doesn't suddenly show up, that tough Mr Shui Ta!

THE SISTER-IN-LAW *laughs*.

THE BROTHER (*reaching for a cigarette*). You won't mind the odd one now, will you?

THE HUSBAND. Bound not to.

All help themselves. THE BROTHER *passes a jug of wine around.*

THE NEPHEW. It's on the cousin!

THE GRANDFATHER (*earnestly to* SHEN TE). How do you do?

SHEN TE, *bewildered by the belated greeting, bows. She holds* THE CARPENTER'*s bill in her hand.*

THE WIFE. What about a little song to entertain our hostess?

THE NEPHEW. Uncle to start!

They sing The Smoke Song.

THE HUSBAND. Years ago, before the years' snow turned my hair white,
I hoped to make my way in life by native wit.
Today I know that no amount of wits suffice
To fill the belly of a poor unfortunate.
    And so I said: drop it!
    See the grey smoke
    Twisting in thin air:
    You'll go the same way too.

THE WIFE. I saw the honest and hardworking type lose out,
And so I tried the other, crooked way of vice.
But that also leads the likes of us to ruin,
So I can't offer any cleverer advice
    Than this: drop it!
    See the grey smoke
    Twisting in thin air:
    You'll go the same way too.

THE NIECE. Those who are old, I hear, have nothing left to hope for
Because hope needs time, and their time, alas, is short.
But the young like us, I hear, the gate is open for,

What it opens on, though, so I hear, is nought.
  So I also say: drop it!
  See the grey smoke
  Twisting in thin air:
  You'll go the same way too.

THE NEPHEW. Where did the wine come from?

THE SISTER-IN-LAW. He popped the sack of tobacco.

THE HUSBAND. What? That tobacco was all we had left! We didn't even touch it when we had no place to stay! You pig!

THE BROTHER. My wife's shivering and you're calling me a pig!

You've drunk some of that yourself! Give that jug over here!

They fight. The shelves with cigarettes fall over.

SHEN TE (*beseechingly*). Oh please spare my shop, don't break everything! It was a present from the gods! Take anything you want, but don't destroy it!

THE WIFE (*sceptically*). This shop's not as big as I thought. Perhaps we shouldn't have told auntie and the others about it. If they turn up, it'll get rather cramped in here.

THE SISTER-IN-LAW. Our hostess seems to have grown a little cooler towards us as well!

Voices from outside and a knock at the door.

Calls off: Open up! It's us!

THE WIFE. Is that you, auntie? What are we going to do?

SHEN TE. My lovely shop! My hope! No sooner opened than it's no longer a shop.

To the audience.
The little lifeboat
Is quickly swamped:
Too many of the shipwrecked
Thrust themselves upon it.

Calls from outside: Open up!

Interlude

Under a Bridge

The water-seller is crouching on the river bank

WANG (*looking around*). All quiet. I've been in hiding now for four days. They can't find me so long as I keep my eyes open. I've purposely fled along their route. On the second day they crossed this bridge, I heard their footsteps overhead. They must be miles away by now. I'm safe here.

He lies back and falls asleep. Music. The slope becomes transparent, and the gods appear.

WANG (*lifts his arm in front of his face, as though to ward off a blow*). Don't say anything, I know! None of the people I found would have you in their homes! There, now you know! Now pass on!

FIRST GOD. No, you did find someone. They came when you were gone. They gave us shelter for the night, they watched over our sleep, and they lit our way out in the morning, as we were leaving. You assured us they were good, and you were right.

WANG. So it was Shen Te who took you in?

THIRD GOD. Naturally.

WANG. And I, faint-hearted man, ran off! Just because I thought: she can't come back. Because she doesn't have any money, I thought she'll not come.

THE GODS.
   O feeble!
   O well-intentioned but feeble man!
   Where there is indigence, he thinks there can be no goodness!
   Where there is risk, he thinks there is no bravery!
   O weakness that doesn't believe in virtue!
   O precipitate judgment! O facile despair!

WANG. I am deeply ashamed, O Enlightened Ones!

FIRST GOD. And now, water-seller, do us the favour of running back to the city and calling on the good Shen Te, so that you may report on her progress to us. She is doing well now. She is said to have got money to buy a small business, so that she is able to follow the stirrings of her kind heart. Encourage her in her goodness, because no one can remain good, unless goodness is required of them. For our part, we will go on looking, and find other people like our good person of Sichuan, to put an end to the chorus of opinion that says it is impossible for good people to live in our world.

They vanish.

Scene Two

The Tobacco Shop

Sleeping people 'all over the shop'. The lamp has been left on all night. A knock at the door.

THE WIFE (*gets up, drunk with sleep*). Shen Te! There's someone at the door. Where has she got to?

THE NEPHEW. She's probably out getting breakfast. It's on the cousin!

THE WIFE *laughs, and shuffles over to the door. Enter a young gentleman* [SHUI TA], *followed by* THE CARPENTER.

SHUI TA. I am the cousin.

THE WIFE (*thunderstruck*). You're what?

SHUI TA. My name is Shui Ta.

THE GUESTS (*shaking each other awake*). – It's the cousin! – But that was a joke, she doesn't have one! – But here's someone who says he's the cousin! – Incredible, at this time of the morning!

THE NEPHEW. If you're the cousin of our hostess, then get us something for breakfast!

SHUI TA (*turning off the lamp*). The first customers will be along soon, so please get dressed so that I can open up my shop.

THE HUSBAND. Your shop? I thought it belonged to our friend Shen Te? (SHUI TA *shakes his head.*) What, are you saying it's not her shop?

THE SISTER-IN-LAW. So she's deceived us? Where has she got to anyway?

SHUI TA. She is unable to be here. She asks me to say that she cannot do anything more for you, now that I am here.

THE WIFE (*shaken*). And we thought she was a good person!

THE NEPHEW. Don't believe him! Look for her!

THE HUSBAND. Yes, let's do that. (*He organises them.*) You and you and you and you form a search party. We'll stay here with grandfather and hold the fort. In the meantime the boy can get us something to eat. (*To* THE BOY.) Do you see the cake-stand on the corner? Creep up on it and grab a shirtful!

SISTER-IN-LAW. And take some of those little light-coloured cakes too!

THE HUSBAND. But don't let the baker catch you! And steer clear of the policeman!

THE BOY *nods and goes. The others finish getting dressed.*

SHUI TA. Won't the theft of these cakes damage the reputation of the shop which has sheltered you?

THE NEPHEW. Don't worry about him, we'll find her soon enough. Then she can tell him where to get off.

Exeunt THE NEPHEW, THE BROTHER, THE SISTER-IN-LAW *and* THE NIECE.

THE SISTER-IN-LAW (*on her way out*). Leave us some breakfast, won't you?

SHUI TA (*calmly*). They won't find her. My cousin regrets that she is unable to extend her hospitality indefinitely. There are simply too many of you! This is a tobacco shop, and it is Miss Shen Te's only means of support.

THE HUSBAND. Such words could never have passed the lips of our Shen Te!

SHUI TA. You may be right. (*To* THE CARPENTER.) Unhappily, poverty in this city is quite simply too great for a single person to combat effectively. It is regrettable that nothing has changed in the eleven hundred years since someone composed the following verses:

The governor, asked what was necessary to help the homeless
In our town in winter, answered:
A blanket ten thousand feet long,
Which would simply cover the suburbs.

He sets to work, tidying the shop.

THE CARPENTER. I see you are making an effort to put the affairs of your cousin in order. There is a small debt still outstanding on the shelving, I have witnesses. Fifty silver dollars.

SHUI TA (*taking the bill out of his pocket, not unkindly*). Don't you think fifty silver dollars is a little excessive?

THE CARPENTER. No. Nor can I make any reduction in the amount. I have a wife and children to feed.

SHUI TA (*harshly*). How many children?

THE CARPENTER. Four.

SHUI TA. Then I offer you four silver dollars.

The man laughs.

THE CARPENTER. Are you mad? These shelves are walnut!

SHUI TA. Then remove them.

THE CARPENTER. What do you mean?

SHUI TA. They are too expensive. I'm asking you to remove the walnut shelving.

THE WIFE. What an operator! (*She laughs too.*)

THE CARPENTER (*uncertainly*). I demand that Miss Shen Te be brought. She seems to be a better person than you.

SHUI TA. I daresay. She's broke.

THE CARPENTER (*resolutely picking up some shelving and carrying it over to the door*). Then you can stack your tobacco goods on the floor! Please yourself.

SHUI TA (*to* THE HUSBAND). Give him a hand!

THE HUSBAND (*picks up some shelving and carries it over to the door, grinning*). Let's get these shelves out of here!

THE CARPENTER. You son of a bitch! Do you want my family to starve?

SHUI TA. I'll offer you two silver dollars, because I'd prefer not to stack my tobacco goods on the floor.

THE CARPENTER. You said four!

SHUI TA *looks indifferently out of the window.* THE HUSBAND *sets about carrying the shelving out of the door.*

THE CARPENTER. Don't bash it against the door-frame, you half-wit! (*Desperately.*) But they've been made to measure! They fit in this hole and nowhere else. The boards have been sawn up, sir!

SHUI TA. Precisely. That's why I'm only offering you two silver dollars. Because the boards have been sawn up.

THE WIFE *squeals with delight.*

THE CARPENTER (*suddenly crumpling*). I can't compete with that. Keep the shelves. Pay whatever you want.

SHUI TA. Two silver dollars.

He puts two coins down on the counter. THE CARPENTER *picks them up.*

THE HUSBAND (*carrying the shelves back inside*). Good enough for a load of sawn-up boards!

THE CARPENTER. Good enough to get drunk on, with luck! (*Exit.*)

THE HUSBAND. That got rid of him!

THE WIFE (*drying tears of laughter*). 'But they're walnut!' 'Take them away!' 'Fifty silver dollars! I've got four children!' 'I'll give you four!' 'But they've been sawn up!' 'Two silver dollars then!' That's the way to deal with them!

SHUI TA. Yes. (*Seriously.*) Now go away!

THE HUSBAND. Us?

SHUI TA. Yes, you. You're thieves and spongers. If you leave quickly, without wasting your time arguing, you may get away.

THE HUSBAND. The best course is not to reply at all. Don't start shouting on an empty stomach. I wonder what's keeping the boy?

SHUI TA. Yes, where is he? I told you I don't want him in my shop with stolen cakes. (*Suddenly shouting.*) For the last time: Get out!

They remain seated.

(*Once more perfectly calm.*) As you please.

He goes over to the door and greets someone outside very respectfully. THE POLICEMAN *appears in the doorway.*

SHUI TA. Am I right in thinking I'm speaking to the district constable?

THE POLICEMAN. That's correct, Mr . . .

SHUI TA. Shui Ta. (*They smile at one another.*) Pleasant weather we're having!

THE POLICEMAN. Perhaps a shade too warm.

THE HUSBAND (*quietly to* THE WIFE). If he keeps him talking till the boy gets back, we're sunk.

He tries to make signs to SHUI TA.

SHUI TA (*ignoring him*). When judging the weather, it makes a difference if one is in a cool bar, or on a dusty street.

THE POLICEMAN. A very material difference.

THE WIFE (*to* THE HUSBAND). Calm down! The boy won't come while the policeman is standing in the doorway.

SHUI TA. Why don't you step inside for a moment? It's a little cooler here. My cousin and I have opened a shop. I should like to say that we attach great importance to maintaining a close understanding with the authorities.

THE POLICEMAN (*steps inside*). Very good of you, Mr Shui Ta, it actually is cooler in here.

THE HUSBAND (*quietly*). He's deliberately brought him indoors so the boy won't see him standing there.

SHUI TA. Some guests. Distant acquaintances of my cousin's, they tell me. They are passing through town. (*The parties bow to one another.*) We were just saying goodbye.

THE HUSBAND (*thickly*). Yes, well it's time we were off.

SHUI TA. I'll inform my cousin that you thank her for the lodgings, and had no time to await her return.

From the street, noise and shouts of 'Stop, thief!'

THE POLICEMAN. What's going on?

THE BOY *is standing in the doorway. Little cakes and buns are spilling out of his shirt.* THE WIFE *is desperately waving to him to clear off. He turns to run out.*

THE POLICEMAN. Oi you, stop! (*He grabs him.*) Where did you get those cakes from?

THE BOY. Over there.

THE POLICEMAN. Stole them, I suppose.

THE WIFE. It was nothing to do with us. The boy acted on his own initiative. You scamp!

THE POLICEMAN. Mr Shui Ta, can you shed any light on this incident?

SHUI TA *says nothing.*

Right, you're all coming back to the station with me.

SHUI TA. I am scandalised that such a thing should happen in my shop.

THE WIFE. But he stood there and watched as the boy set off!

SHUI TA. I can assure you, Mr Officer, that I would hardly have invited you in, if I'd been intent on covering up a crime.

THE POLICEMAN. That stands to reason. You'll understand, though, Mr Shui Ta, that it's my duty to take these people away for questioning. (SHUI TA *bows*.)

SHUI TA. One last thing: Don't you want to take your sacks with you?

THE HUSBAND (*looking at him imploringly*). What sacks? We never brought any sacks with us.

SHUI TA (*slowly*). Ah, then my cousin must have been mistaken, or I've misunderstood her. (*To* THE POLICEMAN.) That's fine then.

THE POLICEMAN. Away with you! (*He drives them out.*)

THE GRANDFATHER (*ceremoniously, on the doorstep*). Good morning.

All exeunt except for SHUI TA. SHUI TA *quickly goes back, and brings a sack up to the front.*

SHUI TA (*showing the sack to the audience*). Opium. (*He hears someone coming, and quickly hides the sack.*)

THE POLICEMAN (*returning*). I've handed the riff-raff over to a colleague of mine. Excuse me for coming in again. I want to thank you on behalf of the police.

SHUI TA. It is I who am indebted to you, sir.

THE POLICEMAN (*with seeming casualness*). There was something said about some sacks earlier. That riff-raff didn't leave anything here, did they, Mr Shui Ta?

SHUI TA. Not a thing. Do you smoke?

THE POLICEMAN (*pocketing a couple of cigars*). Mr Shui Ta, I must confess to you that we at the police first viewed this shop with mixed feelings, but your decisive appearance on the side of public order just now has shown the kind of man you are. We are always quick to identify parties in whom the law can put its trust. I hope you'll be staying here among us.

SHUI TA. I'm afraid I can't stay, and I won't be back either. I was only passing through, and was able to help my cousin out in an emergency. Soon she will be left to her own devices once more. I am very concerned as to what will become of her.

THE POLICEMAN. Why not find a husband for her?

SHUI TA. A husband?

THE POLICEMAN (*enthusiastically*). Yes, why not? She's a good match. Between you and me, Mr Shu Fu the barber next door, a man who owns twelve houses, and has only one elderly wife, indicated to me yesterday that he takes a flattering interest in the young lady. He even inquired as to the state of her fortunes. That's proof of genuine feeling . . .

SHUI TA (*cautiously*). It's not a bad idea. Might you be able to arrange a meeting?

THE POLICEMAN. I think so. Of course, it will have to be done with some delicacy. Mr Shu Fu is a sensitive plant. I would suggest a chance encounter in front of the teahouse by the lake. There is a bathing-hut there, as I know because I was able to secure an arrest there only last week. Miss Shen Te might be admiring the goldfish and in her rapture let fall a remark such as . . . well, such as?

SHUI TA. Look at the lovely goldfish.

THE POLICEMAN. Brilliant! And Mr Shu Fu might say in reply, for instance . . .

SHUI TA. I see only the beautiful face reflected in the waters, Miss.

THE POLICEMAN. Perfect. I'll go and have a word with Mr Shu Fu right away. Don't imagine, Mr Shui Ta, that the authorities aren't without the finer feelings where an honest entrepreneur is concerned.

SHUI TA. I was starting to feel rather pessimistic about the future of this little shop, which was a gift from the gods to my cousin. But now I see a solution. Still it's frightening that life demands so much good fortune, so many ideas and such good friends.

Scene Three

The City Park in the Evening

A young man [YANG SUN] in ragged clothes watches an aeroplane which seems to be flying in a high arc over the park. He pulls a rope out of his pocket, and starts looking around. He is heading for a large willow tree, when a couple of prostitutes accost him. One is already old, the other is THE NIECE from the family of eight.

THE NIECE. Good evening, young sir? D'you want business, darling?

YANG SUN. I might do, ladies. If you buy me something to eat.

OLD PROSTITUTE. You must be crazy. (*To* THE NIECE.) Let's go. Don't waste your time on him. He's the unemployed airman.

THE NIECE. But there won't be another man in the park now, and it's about to rain.

OLD PROSTITUTE. Maybe there will.

They pass on. Looking around, YANG SUN takes his rope out again, and throws it over a branch of the willow. But he is disturbed again. The two prostitutes come back quickly. They don't see him.

THE NIECE. It's going to be a real downpour.

SHEN TE *strolls by.*

OLD PROSTITUTE. Look, there's that bitch! She brought misfortune on you and your family!

THE NIECE. It wasn't her. It was her cousin. She took us in, and later she offered to pay for the cakes. I've no quarrel with her.

OLD PROSTITUTE. But I do. (*Loudly.*) Ah, there's our fine sister with the shower of gold! She owns her own shop now, but she's still trying to pinch customers from us.

SHEN TE. Don't bite my head off. I'm only going to the teahouse by the lake.

THE NIECE. So is it true that you're having to marry the barber then?

SHEN TE. Yes, it's him I'm going to meet there.

YANG SUN (*impatiently*). Get along with you, you trulls! Can't a fellow enjoy a moment's peace out here?

OLD PROSTITUTE. You shut your face!

Exeunt the two prostitutes.

YANG SUN (*calling after them*). Vampires! (*To the audience.*) Even in this remote spot you find them tirelessly hunting for prey, even in the bushes and when it's about to rain they're desperately looking for customers.

SHEN TE (*angrily*). Why are you calling them names? (*She sees the rope.*) Oh.

YANG SUN. What are you looking at?

SHEN TE. What are you doing with that rope?

YANG SUN. Walk on, sister, walk on! I've got no money, not even a copper coin. And if I did, I wouldn't spend it on you, I'd buy myself a cup of water first.

It starts raining.

SHEN TE. What are you doing with that rope? You mustn't!

YANG SUN. It's none of your business. Get lost!

SHEN TE. It's raining!

YANG SUN. Don't think you can get under my tree.

SHEN TE (*stays motionless in the rain*). No.

YANG SUN. Forget it, sister, it's no good. I wouldn't have you anyway. You're too ugly. Your legs are crooked.

SHEN TE. That's not true.

YANG SUN. Don't show me them, please! All right, dammit. Come on, get under the tree out of the rain!

She slowly goes under the tree and sits down.

SHEN TE. Why did you want to do that?

YANG SUN. Do you really want to know? All right then, I'll tell you, so I'm rid of you. (*Pause.*) Do you know what a pilot is?

SHEN TE. Yes, I saw some pilots once in a teahouse.

YANG SUN. No you didn't. You just saw a few idiots in leather helmets mouthing off. Men with no ear for engines, and no feel for their machines. The kind of thing that only gets to go up in a plane because it can bribe the manager of the hangar. Try telling one of them to drop two thousand feet through the clouds, and then to pick her up with a touch on the stick, and he'll tell you: it's not in my contract. Anyone who doesn't land his crate like it was his own butt is no pilot but a fool. I'm a pilot. But I'm also the biggest fool of all because I read all the textbooks on flying at pilot school in Peking. But there was one page in one book that I didn't read, and on that page it said that no more pilots were required. So I'm a pilot without a plane, a mail-pilot with no mail. But you can't imagine what that's like.

SHEN TE. I think I can.

YANG SUN. No, I'm telling you you can't, so you can't.

SHEN TE (*half laughing, half crying*). When we were little, we had a pet crane with a lame wing. He was a friendly bird, and didn't mind us playing with him and he used to go swaggering about after us, and squawk crossly when we left him behind. But in the autumn, and in spring, when the great migrations passed over the village, it made him very restless, and I understood how he felt.

YANG SUN. Don't cry.

SHEN TE. No.

YANG SUN. It's bad for the complexion.

She wipes her tears away with her sleeve. Leaning against the tree, not looking at her, he reaches down and touches her face.

You can't even wipe your face properly.

He wipes it with a piece of sacking. Pause.

If you have to sit here and make sure I don't hang myself, you might at least say something.

SHEN TE. I don't know what to say.

YANG SUN. So why do you want to cut me down, sister?

SHEN TE. I'm frightened. I'm sure you only wanted to do it because it was such a grey evening.

> *To the audience.*
> In this our country, and in these times
> We should be rid of dull and gloomy evenings.
> Likewise high bridges over the rivers,
> Also the hour before the dawn appears
> And the freezing winter time each year –
> All of these are fraught with danger.
> For man's unhappiness is so intense
> A whispered suggestion would be sufficient cause
> To throw his unbearable life away.

YANG SUN. Tell me about yourself.

SHEN TE. What? I have a little shop.

YANG SUN (*sarcastically*). Oh I see, you're not a streetwalker at all, you have a little shop!

SHEN TE (*firmly*). I have a shop, but before that I used to walk the streets.

YANG SUN. And I take it the shop was a gift from the gods?

SHEN TE. Yes.

YANG SUN. One fine evening they stood there and said: here's some money for you?

SHEN TE (*laughing quietly*). One morning, in fact.

YANG SUN. You're not very amusing, are you?

SHEN TE (*after a pause*). I can play the lute a bit, and I can imitate people's voices. (*In a deep voice she copies a dignitary.*) 'Oh how stupid of me, I seem to have left home without my money bags.' And then I got the shop. The first thing I did was give away my lute. Now, I said to myself, I can be silent and it won't matter.

I am rich, I said.
I am alone, I sleep alone.
For a whole year, I said,

I will have nothing to do with men.

YANG SUN. But now you're off to get married, eh? The fellow in the teahouse by the lake?

SHEN TE *says nothing.*

YANG SUN. What do you know about love?

SHEN TE. Everything.

YANG SUN. Nothing, sister. Or did you like it?

SHEN TE. No.

SUN (*strokes her face without looking at her*). Do you like this?

SHEN TE. Yes.

YANG SUN. Easily satisfied, aren't you? What a town!

SHEN TE. Don't you have any friends?

YANG SUN. Heaps of friends, but no one who cares to hear that I still haven't got a job. They make a face as if I was complaining that the sea's full of salt water.

SHEN TE. It is said: to speak without hope is to speak without goodness.

YANG SUN. I have no hope. Five hundred silver dollars would make me a human being. When a letter arrived this morning saying there was a job for me, I reached for the rope. The price tag on the job is 500 dollars.

SHEN TE. Is it a job as a pilot? (*As he nods, she carries on slowly.*) I have a friend, a cousin, who might be able to come up with that kind of money. But he is very cunning and very mean. It would really have to be the last time. But a pilot needs to fly, anyone can see that.

YANG SUN. What are you talking about?

SHEN TE. Can you come to Sandalmakers Lane tomorrow? To the little tobacco shop? If I'm not there, my cousin will be.

YANG SUN (*laughs*). And if your cousin's not there, then there won't be anyone there at all, eh? (*He looks at her.*) Your scarf is the prettiest thing about you.

SHEN TE. Yes? (*Pause.*) I felt a raindrop.

YANG SUN. Really?

SHEN TE. Just between my eyes.

YANG SUN. Nearer to the left or the right?

SHEN TE. Nearer the left.

YANG SUN. Fine. (*After a while, sleepily.*) And you're through
    with men?

SHEN TE (*smiling*). But my legs aren't crooked.

YANG SUN. Maybe not.

SHEN TE. Definitely not.

YANG SUN (*sleepily leaning back against the tree*). But as I haven't
    eaten anything in two days, or drunk anything in one, I
    couldn't love you, sister, if I wanted to.

SHEN TE. I like it in the rain.

> WANG *the Water-seller comes. He sings*: The Song of the
> Waterseller in the Rain.

WANG. I sell water for a living –
    And now it's pissing down like hell.
    Had to walk for miles this morning
    To fill this bucket at the well.
        Water!
    Thirsty and parched
    No one will try it,
    No one pays me,
    And no one buys it.
    (Buy water, you bastards!)

    How I'd love to bung up the sky.
    Once I dreamed the rain just stopped.
    Seven years of dehydration –
    I was selling by the drop!
        Water!
    Water, please! They cried.
    They held out their hands.
    You should have seen their mugs;

Go jump in the lake!
(The bastards' tongues were hanging out!)

(*Laughingly.*)
Now you little weeds are suckling
At the fat breasts of the clouds,
Lying on your backs and chuckling,
And it's my job that's up the spout.
    Water!
Thirsty and parched,
No one will try it,
No one pays me,
No one buys it.
(Buy water, you bastards!)

The rain has stopped. SHEN TE *sees* WANG *and rushes up to him.*

SHEN TE. Oh Wang, are you back? I've got your gear waiting in my room.

WANG. Thank you very much for minding it for me! How are you, Shen Te?

SHEN TE. I'm fine. I've met a very bold and clever man. And I'd like to buy a cupful of your water.

WANG. Why not tip your head back and open your mouth, and you'll have as much water as you want? The will over there is still weeping.

SHEN TE.
But Wang, it's your water I want,
Brought from afar,
Fatiguingly,
And hard to sell because of the rain today.
I want it for the gentleman over there.
He's a pilot. A pilot
Is bolder than other men.
He lives in the society of clouds.
Braving great tempests
He flies through the air
Bringing friends in faraway lands
News of their friends.

WANG. Weren't you going to meet someone in the park who was going to help you?

SHEN TE. Yes, but now I've found someone whom I can help, Wang.

She pays and runs back to YANG SUN *with the cup.*

(*Calling laughingly back to* WANG.) He's fallen asleep. His despair, the rain and I, between us, have tired him out.

Interlude

WANG's *Sleeping Place in a Sewage Pipe*

The water-seller is asleep. Music. The sewage pipe becomes transparent, and the gods appear to the man in a dream.

WANG (*beaming*). I've seen her, Enlightened Ones! She's absolutely unspoilt!

FIRST GOD. That's good news.

WANG. She's in love! I met her new friend. She's really happy.

FIRST GOD. We're pleased to hear that, certainly. May it strengthen her in her determination to do good.

WANG. It's bound to! She does all the good she can.

FIRST GOD. What are these good actions she does? Tell us about them, dear Wang!

WANG. She has a kind word for everyone.

FIRST GOD (*avidly*). Yes. What else?

WANG. It's almost unheard of for anyone to leave her little shop without tobacco, just because they have no money.

FIRST GOD. That's not bad. Now what else?

WANG. She's put up a family of eight!

FIRST GOD (*triumphantly to the* SECOND GOD). Family of eight, eh! (*To* WANG.) Anything further, perchance?

WANG. She bought a cup of water from me even though it was raining.

FIRST GOD. Naturally, all these little good turns. We would have expected nothing less.

WANG. But they cost money. A small shop doesn't make that much.

FIRST GOD. True, true! But a thoughtful gardener performs miracles even with a small plot of ground.

WANG. That's just what she does. Every morning she distributes rice, and that comes to more than half her turnover, believe me!

FIRST GOD (*somewhat disappointed*). I'm not saying anything. It's not bad for a beginning.

WANG. Consider that the times are none too good! The shop got into difficulties, and she had to call in a cousin to help her.

No sooner was there found a sheltered place
Than all the ruffled inhabitants
Of the winter sky flew to it
And fought for room, and the hungry fox bit
Through the thin wall, and the one-legged wolf
Upset the little dish of food.

In short, she could no longer cope with the business on her own. But everyone's agreed that she's a fine lass. They call her: the angel of the suburbs. So much good goes out from her shop! Whatever the carpenter Lin To says!

FIRST GOD. What's that? Does the carpenter Lin To speak ill of her?

WANG. Oh, all he says is that the shelving in the shop hasn't been paid for in full.

SECOND GOD. What's that? A carpenter hasn't been paid? In Shen Te's shop? How could she allow that to happen?

WANG. I suppose she didn't have the money!

SECOND GOD. Never mind that, you meet your liabilities. Even the appearance of unfairness should be avoided. The letter of the law must be obeyed, and then its spirit.

WANG. But it was her cousin who was responsible, Enlightened One, not herself.

SECOND GOD. Then this cousin should be banned from the premises in future!

WANG (*dejectedly*). I understand, Enlightened One. But let me say on Shen Te's behalf that the cousin has a reputation as a respectable businessman. Even the police esteem him.

FIRST GOD. Well, let's not condemn her cousin out of hand. I must confess, I don't understand the first thing about business, perhaps one should find out what the norm is. But then again, business! Is that really necessary? Everyone's in business nowadays! Were the Seven Good Kings businessmen? Did the Just Kung sell fish? What does business have to do with an upright and dignified life?

SECOND GOD (*rather sniffy*). At any rate it shouldn't happen again.

He turns to leave. The other two gods do likewise.

THIRD GOD (*the last of the three, apologetically*). Excuse the harsh tone today! We're overtired, and haven't been sleeping properly. The lodgings we've had! The well-to-do send us on to the destitute, and the destitute don't have very much room.

THE GODS (*exiting, crossly*). Weak, the best of them! – No great success there! – Poor show, poor show! – She means well of course, but it's not much to write home about! – She ought at least . . .

They are no longer audible.

WANG (*calling after them*). Don't be harsh with her, Enlightened Ones! Don't expect too much to start off with!

Interlude

Before the Curtain

SHEN TE *appears, carrying* SHUI TA's *mask and suit, and sings*
The Song of the Defencelessness of the Gods and the Good

SHEN TE.
>In our country
>The useful man needs luck. Only
>If he finds strong backers
>Can he develop his usefulness.
>The good
>Cannot help themselves, and the gods are powerless to assist
>   them.
>>Why are the gods not equipped with guns and tanks
>>With bombs and with shells, and with air and sea power,
>>To succour the good and destroy the bad?
>>It would be to their advantage and to ours.

She puts on SUI TA's *suit, and takes a few steps in his gait.*

>The good
>In our country cannot long remain good.
>Where there's nothing on the plates, the hungry come to blows.
>Ah, the commandments of the gods
>Are unavailing against want.
>>Why do the gods not appear in our midst,
>>And smile as they hand out the fruits of the earth,
>>And so permit those strengthened by bread and wine
>>To live together on a friendly, decent basis?

She puts on SHUI TA's *mask, and carries on singing in his voice:*

>To obtain a square meal
>Requires as much ruthlessness as to found an empire.
>There's no helping a single beggar
>Without trampling on a dozen others.
>>Why do the gods up on high not say aloud
>>That they owe the good a good world to inhabit?
>>Why don't they stand with the good and shout
>>'Take aim! Fire!' and suffer no suffering.

Scene Four

The Tobacco Shop

SHUI TA *is sitting behind the counter reading a newspaper. He is paying not the slightest attention to MRS SHIN, who is cleaning, and talking at the same time.*

MRS SHIN. I'm not one to gossip, Mr Shui Ta, but I think you should know what's going on. Tongues are wagging about Miss Shen Te staying out all night – it's all the riff-raff gathering outside the shop early in the morning to get a bowl of rice – and it's not doing the reputation of the shop any good at all.

> *Not receiving any reply, she eventually goes outside with her bucket.*

A VOICE (*from outside*). Is this Miss Shen Te's shop?

MRS SHIN'S VOICE. Yes it is. But her cousin's in today.

> SHUI TA *walks with* SHEN TE's *light steps to a mirror, and is about to arrange his hair, when he recognises his error in the mirror. He turns away softly laughing to himself. Enter* YANG SUN. *Behind him the nosy* MRS SHIN. *She passes him and goes into the back room.*

YANG SUN. My name is Yang Sun. (SHUI TA *bows.*) Is Shen Te around?

SHUI TA. No, she's not here.

YANG SUN. But I think she's told you about us. (*He starts taking stock of the shop.*) A bona fide shop! I thought that was just talk. (*He peers contentedly into little boxes and china jars.*) Nifty, very nifty. (*He helps himself to a cigar and* SHUI TA *offers him a light.*) Do you think we could manage to get 500 silver dollars out of this shop?

SHUI TA (*surprised, but also amused*). Might I ask whether you are proposing to sell it immediately?

YANG SUN. Do we have 500 in cash? (SHUI TA *shakes his head.*) So we have to sell.

SHUI TA. It may have been a little precipitate of her to promise you the money. It could cost her the shop. It is said: Haste is the wind that blows down the scaffolding.

YANG SUN. I need the money fast or not at all. And the girl's not the type to hang around. Between you and me: Not in other respects either.

SHUI TA. Well.

YANG SUN. Yes, well.

SHUI TA. May I ask you what the 500 silver dollars would be used for?

YANG SUN. Yes. I can see this is turning into a cross-examination. The hangar-manager in Peking, a friend of mine from flying school, can get me a job if I slip him 500 silver dollars.

SHUI TA. Isn't the amount unusually large?

YANG SUN. No. He has to prove negligence against one of his pilots, and the man has a large family, and is therefore extremely conscientious. You see what I mean. This is in confidence, and Shen Te doesn't need to know about it.

SHUI TA. Perhaps not. One question: won't the hangar manager sell *you* down the river next month?

YANG SUN. Not me. You won't catch me being negligent. I've been out of a job for long enough.

SHUI TA (*nods*). The hungry dog pulls the cart home the faster.(*He looks at him appraisingly for a while.*) The responsibility is very great. Mr Yang Sun, you're asking my cousin to give up her small property and all her friends in the city, and to put herself entirely in your hands. May I take it you intend to marry her?

YANG SUN. That's a step I'd be prepared to take.

SHUI TA. Then isn't it a pity to sell the shop at a knock-down price? If you're in a hurry to sell, you won't get very much money for it. Mightn't you be interested in taking over a tobacco business?

YANG SUN. Me? Yang Sun, the pilot, standing behind the

counter: 'Would Sir like a strong cigar, or something a little more mellow?' That's no work for a Yang Sun, not in this century!

SHUI TA. May I ask, is flying well paid?

YANG SUN (*takes a letter out of his pocket*). One hundred and fifty silver dollars a month sir! See the letter for yourself. Here is the stamp, and the postmark. Peking.

SHUI TA. One hundred and fifty silver dollars? That's a lot.

YANG SUN. Do you expect me to fly for the fun of it?

SHUI TA. It seems to be a very good job. Now, Mr Yang Sun, my cousin has asked me to help you secure this job as a pilot, which means so much to you. From the point of view of my cousin, I see no reason why she should not follow the promptings of her heart. She is fully entitled to experience the joys of love. I am prepared to turn all this to cash. Here comes the tobacco dealer, Mrs Mi Tsu, whose advice I have asked for on the sale.

MRS MI TSU (*enters*). Good day, Mr Shui Ta. Is it true that you want to sell the shop?

SHUI TA. Mrs Mi Tsu, my cousin is minded to marry, and her intended (*He presents* YANG SUN.) Mr Yang Sun, is taking her to Peking, where they will embark on a new life together. If I can get enough money for my tobacco, I'll sell.

MRS MI TSU. How much money do you need?

YANG SUN. Five hundred on the table.

MRS MI TSU. How much did your tobacco cost?

SHUI TA. My cousin brought it for 1000 silver dollars, and only a very little has been sold.

MRS MI TSU. One thousand silver dollars! She's been taken for a ride. I'll tell you what: I'll give you 300 silver dollars for the whole shop if I can have vacant possession the day after tomorrow.

YANG SUN. We'll let you have that, of course, but you'll have to do better than 300. (*Like an auctioneer.*) First class tobacco, recently purchased, excellent condition, factory price of 1000 dollars. Plus the entire furnishings of the shop, and the goodwill secured by attractive owner. All this, owing to special circumstances, knocked down for just 500 dollars! Terrific opportunity. You're a woman of sound sense, you understand life, I can see that. (*He fondles her.*) And you understand love too, I can sense that. 'Flog off the shop for less than what you paid for it, shotgun wedding' – that kind of thing is a perfect opportunity for business people.

MRS MI TSU (*not unreceptive but firmly*). Three hundred dollars.

YANG SUN (*takes SHUI TA aside*). It's not enough, but better than nothing, eh? Three hundred down, that's a start.

SHUI TA (*alarmed*). But we won't get the job for 300.

YANG SUN. No, but what would I do with the shop anyway?

SHUI TA. Yes, but then everything's gone, what will you live on?

YANG SUN. But I'll have 300 dollars. (*To the tobacco dealer.*) We'll do it. Lock, stock and barrel for 300 and no more messing. When can we have the money by?

MRS MI TSU. Right away. (*She pulls banknotes out of her pocket.*) Here are 300 dollars because I'm anxious to do my bit for young romance.

YANG SUN (*to SHUI TA*). Put 300 down in the contract. I see Shen Te's signature is already on it.

SHUI TA *writes in the figure and hands the contract to the tobacco dealer.* YANG SUN *takes the money out of her hand.*

MRS MI TSU. Good day, Mr Yang Sun; good day, Mr Shui Ta. Give my regards to Miss Shen Te. (*Exit.*)

YANG SUN (*sits down at the counter exhausted*). Done it, old man!

SHUI TA. But it's not enough.

YANG SUN. That's right. We're 200 short. You'll have to raise that from somewhere.

SHUI TA. How am I going to do that, short of stealing it?

YANG SUN. Your cousin seemed to think you were the man to raise the whole sum.

SHUI TA. Perhaps I am. (*Slowly.*) I'm assuming that Shen Te's future happiness is at stake here. It is said that a person must be good to himself and his sympathy extend to himself also.

YANG SUN. So you'll take care of it. Hey, I'm going to fly!

SHUI TA (*bows, smiling*). A pilot must fly. (*Casually.*) You've got enough money for the two of you to go to Peking, and make a start?

YANG SUN. Sure.

SHUI TA. How much is that?

YANG SUN. Well, I'll get it together even if it means stealing it!

SHUI TA. I see, so this sum needs to be raised as well?

YANG SUN. Don't freak out, man. I'll make it to Peking.

SHUI TA. But it can't be that cheap for two people.

YANG SUN. Who said anything about two? I'm leaving the girl here. She would just be a millstone round my neck in the early days.

SHUI TA. I see.

YANG SUN. Why are you looking at me as if I was a leaky petrol tank? You have to reach for the stars.

SHUI TA. And what's my cousin going to live off?

YANG SUN. Can't you help her out?

SHUI TA. I'll do my best. (*Pause.*) I would like you to give the 300 dollars into my safe keeping, Mr Yang Sun, until such time as you can produce two tickets to Peking.

YANG SUN. Don't you trust me then?

SHUI TA. I trust no one.

YANG SUN. Nor me.

They stare at one another.

My dear brother-in-law, I wish you wouldn't involve yourself in the private affairs of two lovers. (*Stands up.*) I can see we don't understand one another. I shall have to turn to the girl for the remaining 200.

SHUI TA (*unconvinced*). Do you really think she'll sacrifice everything for your sake, when you're not even thinking of taking her with you?

YANG SUN. She will. Even then.

SHUI TA. And you're not afraid of my opposition?

YANG SUN. My dear sir!

SHUI TA. You seem to forget that she's a rational human being.

YANG SUN (*droll*). I have always been puzzled by certain people's opinion of their female relatives, and their receptiveness to sound advice. Have you never heard of the power of love before, or of fleshly longings? You want her to be sensible? She has no common sense! The poor creature has been abused all her life! I have only to lay my hand on her shoulder and say: 'You're coming with me', and she'll hear bells, and not recognise her own mother.

SHUI TA (*pained*). Mr Yang Sun!

YANG SUN. Mr Whateveryourname is!

SHUI TA. My cousin is devoted to you, because . . . .

YANG SUN. Let's say because it's my hands on her tits. Shove that in your pipe and smoke it!

He helps himself to another cigar, shoves a couple more in his pocket and finally tucks the whole box of them under his arm.

And now I'm going to wait outside until she comes home, and don't worry if she gets in a bit late tonight, we'll be having supper together and discussing the missing two hundred. (*Exit.*)

MRS SHIN (*sticking her head out of the back room*). What a charming character!

SHUI TA (*cries out*). The shop's gone! He doesn't love her! I'm lost! (*He starts pacing about like a caged beast, repeating over and over* 'The shop's gone!' *until he suddenly stops and addresses* MRS SHIN.) Shin, you grew up in the gutter, and so did I.

Are we reckless? No. Are we without the required measure of brutality? No. I'm prepared to grab you by the throat and shake you until you spit out the coin you stole from me, and you know it. The times are vile, this town is hell, but we flatten ourselves against the smooth walls and we climb. Then one of us is overtaken by disaster: he's in love. That's it, he's finished. A moment of weakness, and he's done for. How are we to free ourselves of *every* weakness, especially this most fatal one of all, love? Love is too costly! It's impossible! Then again, tell me, can one live and be forever on one's guard? What kind of world is that?

Caresses turn to strangling.
The sigh of love becomes a cry of fear.
Why are the vultures circling?
There's a woman going to meet her man!

Bring Mr Shu Fu the barber right away. (MRS SHIN *runs off.*)

SHUI TA *paces about again, until* SHU FU *appears, followed by* MRS SHIN, *who however has to withdraw following a gesture of* SHU FU's.

SHUI TA (*hastens towards him*). My dear sir, I have heard a report that you have expressed a certain interest in my cousin. Permit me to dispense with the usual discretion and decorum – the young woman is in very great danger.

SHU FU. Oh!

SHUI TA. A few hours ago the owner of her own shop, my cousin is now little more than a beggar. Mr Shu Fu, the shop is ruined.

SHU FU. Mr Shui Ta, the charm of Miss Shen Te consists not in the goodness of her shop, but in the goodness of her heart. The name by which the young lady is known in this district says it all: The angel of the suburbs.

SHUI TA. My dear sir, this goodness has cost my cousin three hundred silver dollars in a single day: it must be stopped.

SHU FU. Permit me to express a different opinion: disregard this one unfortunate incident: her goodness must on no account be stopped. It is in the nature of the young lady to do good.

What is the feeding of four people that I witness with emotion every morning? Why does she not feed four hundred? I hear she is desperate to find shelter for a few homeless people. My houses behind the stockyard are empty. They are at her disposal. And so on and so forth. Mr Shui Ta, might I hope that such ideas which have come to me in the last few days, might find hearing with Miss Shen Te?

SHUI TA. Mr Shu Fu, she will be lost in admiration at such ideas.

SHU FU. Over dinner in a small but select restaurant.

SHUI TA. With all discretion. I will hasten to notify my cousin. She will be sensible. She is deeply distressed about the shop, which she sees as a present from the gods. Would you kindly wait a moment? (*Exit into the back room.*)

MRS SHIN (*puts her head through the door*). Are congratulations in order?

SHU FU. They are. Mrs Shin, would you tell Miss Shen Te's protégés today on my behalf that they may be assured of shelter in my houses behind the stockyard. (*She nods and grins.*)

(*Rising, to the audience.*) What do you think, ladies and gentlemen? Can one do more? Can one be more selfless? More sensitive? More farsighted? A little dinner! All kinds of vulgar notions enter one's mind when one hears that. But nothing of the sort will happen. No contact, not even an apparently acccidental one, while passing the salt! There will be an exchange of ideas. Two souls will meet over the vase of flowers on the table, white chrysanthemums I think. (*He makes a note of it.*) No, this is no exploitation of an unhappy predicament, no taking advantage of a disappointed party. Help and support will be offered, but almost silently. At the most they may be acknowledged by a glance, a glance that may mean more.

MRS SHIN. So everything went according to plan, Mr Shu Fu?

SHU FU. Oh, entirely according to plan! There are going to be changes in this area. A certain party has been given their marching orders, and certain attempts on this shop will be foiled. Certain people who don't scruple to threaten the reputation of the most virtuous girl in the city will now have me to deal with. What can you tell me about this Yang Sun?

MRS SHIN. He's the dirtiest, rottenest . . . .

SHU FU. He's nothing at all. He doesn't exist. He doesn't figure, Shin.

Enter YANG SUN.

YANG SUN. What's going on here?

MRS SHIN. Mr Shu Fu, would you like me to call Mr Shui Ta? He doesn't like strangers hanging around the shop.

SHU FU. Miss Shen Te is holding important discussions with Mr Shui Ta, which may not be interrupted.

YANG SUN. What, is she here? I never saw her come in! What discussions? I must be in on this.

SHU FU (*bars him from the back room*). You will have to be patient, sir. I believe I know who you are. Be apprised that Miss Shen Te and I are about to announce our engagement.

YANG SUN. What?

MRS SHIN. That surprised you, didn't it?

SUN *struggles with the barber to gain access to the back room.* SHEN TE *steps out.*

SHU FU. I'm sorry, my dear. Perhaps you could explain to . . .

YANG SUN. What's up, Shen Te? Have you gone mad?

SHEN TE (*out of breath*). Sun, my cousin and Mr Shu Fu have decided that I should listen to Mr Shu Fu's ideas on how to better the lot of the people in the tenements. (*Pause.*). My cousin opposes our relationship.

YANG SUN. And you're going along with him?

SHEN TE. Yes.

Pause.

YANG SUN. Did they tell you I was a bad person?

SHEN TE *says nothing.*

Because perhaps I am, Shen Te. That's why I need you. I'm a squalid person. I've no capital, no manners. But I fight back. Look into my eyes! Can you believe that I wouldn't love you without a dowry? They're forcing you into misery, Shen Te. (*He goes to her. Hushed.*) Look at him! Haven't you got eyes in your head? (*With his hand on her shoulder.*) You poor creature, what were they about to inflict on you now? A forced marriage! But for me, they would have dragged you off to the knackers. Tell me yourself, you would have gone with him, wouldn't you, if I hadn't come?

SHEN TE. Yes.

YANG SUN. A man you don't love.

SHEN TE. Yes.

YANG SUN. Have you forgotten how it rained? Everything?

SHEN TE. No.

YANG SUN. The way you cut me down, bought me a glass of water, promised me money so that I could fly once more?

SHEN TE (*trembling*). What do you want?

YANG SUN. For you to go away with me.

SHEN TE. Forgive me, Mr Shu Fu. I want to go away with Sun.

YANG SUN. Take your scarf, the blue one. (SHEN TE *takes the scarf she wore in the park.*)

We're lovers, you see. (*He takes her to the door.*) Where's the key to the shop? (*He fishes it out of her pocket and gives it to* MRS SHIN.) Leave it on the doorstep when you're finished. Come on, Shen Te!

SHU FU. But this is rape! (*Shouts to the back.*) Mr Shui Ta!

YANG SUN. Tell him to stop shouting.

SHEN TE. Please don't shout for my cousin, Mr Shu Fu. I know he doesn't agree with me. But he's wrong, I feel it. (*To the audience.*)
I want to go with the man I love.
I don't want to calculate the cost.

I don't want to consider whether it's good or not.
I want to go with him I love.

YANG SUN. Yeah, that's right.

They both exeunt.

Interlude

In Front of a Teahouse

SHEN TE *with a little sack under her arm.*

SHEN TE. I have never seen the city so early in the morning. At this hour I usually lie with the blanket pulled over my eyes, afraid of the day. But this morning I have walked among the paper boys, the men who sprinkle the roads with water and the ox-carts carrying fresh produce from the countryside. I was always told that when you were in love, you had your head in the clouds, but the wonderful thing is having your feet on the ground, on the asphalt. I tell you the tenements look like heaps of rubble with little lights burning in them, and the sky is pink and still clear, because there is no dust. I tell you, you're missing out on a lot if you're not in love, and you don't see your Sichuan when it gets up like a dogged old labourer, filling his lungs with cool air, and reaching for his tools. And here is the Teahouse of Felicity, where I am to sell this little sack, so that Sun can fly once more.

Just as she is about to go in, some customers spill out. They are opium addicts, derelicts, shivering and falling about. There is a young man who takes out his wallet, finds it empty and tosses it away. There is a woman vomiting. There is an ugly old man in the company of a very young doped girl.

That's terrible. It's opium that has done this to them.

She looks in horror at her little sack.

This is poison. How could I intend to sell it? It doesn't even belong to me. How could I forget that too? In a storm of emotion I threw myself into Sun's arms once more. I was unable to resist his voice and his caresses. The bad things he said to Shui Ta were without effect on Shen Te. Falling into his embrace, I thought: the gods want me to be good to myself also.

Not let anyone go to ruin,
Not even oneself
To fill everyone with happiness,
Including oneself, that
Is good.

Like a small hurricane heading in the direction of Peking, Sun simply swept away my shop, but he is not a bad person and he loves me. As long as I am by he will do nothing bad. What a man says to other men is of no significance. He wants to make himself appear big and powerful, and rather hard-boiled. But when I tell him what I saw here, he will understand. He would sooner go and work in the cement factory with me, than owe his pilot's job to a dirty deed. Admittedly, he has a great passion for flying. Will I be strong enough to appeal to the good in him? Now, as I go to marry him, I hesitate between joy and fear.

Scene Five

A Private Room in a Cheap Restaurant in the Suburbs

A WAITER *is filling the glasses of the wedding party with wine.* SHEN TE *is standing by the* THE GRANDFATHER, THE SISTER-IN-LAW, THE NIECE *and* THE UNEMPLOYED MAN. *A* PRIEST *is standing in a corner alone. At the front* YANG SUN *is speaking to his mother*, MRS YANG. *He is wearing a dinner jacket.*

YANG SUN. Bad news, mum. She's just blurted out that she can't raise the remaining two hundred.

MRS YANG. What did you reply? Of course, if that's the case, you can't marry her.

YANG SUN. There's no point in discussing it with her, she's so stubborn. I told her to get hold of her cousin.

MRS YANG. But he's the one who wants to marry her off to the barber.

YANG SUN. I've taken care of that particular alliance. The barber's been squashed. Her cousin will soon realise that the shop's gone, and if he doesn't get a move on, there'll be no job either.

MRS YANG. I'll go outside and keep a lookout for him. Go and be with your bride now, Sun!

SHEN TE (*to the audience, pouring wine*). I was not deceived in him. He gave no indication whatever of being disappointed. In spite of the heavy blow of not being able to fly and all that means to him, he is quite cheerful. I love him terribly. (*She beckons* YANG SUN *over to her.*) Sun, you haven't touched glasses with the bride yet!

YANG SUN. What'll we drink to?

SHEN TE. Let's drink to the future.

They drink.

YANG SUN. A future where the bridegroom's dinner jacket won't be borrowed.

SHEN TE. But where the bride's dress still sometimes gets caught in the rain.

YANG SUN. All our wishes!

SHEN TE. May they speedily come true!

MRS YANG (*going out, to* MRS SHIN). I am delighted by my son. I've always told him he could get any girl he set his cap at. Why, he's a qualified mechanic and pilot. And what does he tell me now? I'm marrying for love, mum, he tells me. Money isn't everything. It's a love-match! (*To* THE SISTER-IN-LAW.) It had to happen, didn't it? But it's hard on the mother, very hard. (*Calling back to the* PRIEST.) Not too short, if you please. If you spend as much time on the ceremony as you did on agreeing your fee, then it'll be a worthy occasion. (*To* SHEN TE.) We have to delay a little longer, my love. One of the dearest guests has yet to arrive. (*To all.*) Please excuse me.

Exit.

THE SISTER-IN-LAW. One doesn't mind waiting while there's wine to be drunk.

They sit.

THE UNEMPLOYED MAN. One feels one isn't really missing anything.

YANG SUN (*aloud and jokingly in front of the guests*). Now, before our wedding, I must just put you through a little test. It's not inadvisable in the case of marriages that are so speedily concluded. (*To the guests.*) I have no idea what my wife is like. This is disquieting. For example, are you able to make five cups of tea from three tea leaves?

SHEN TE. No.

YANG SUN. So, I shan't be getting any tea then. Can you sleep on a straw mat the size of the priest's prayer book?

SHEN TE. With you?

YANG SUN. Alone.

SHEN TE. Then I can't.

YANG SUN. I am appalled to discover the kind of person my betrothed is.

All laugh. MRS YANG *appears in the doorway behind* SHEN TE. *By shrugging her shoulders, she indicates to* YANG SUN *that the expected guest is nowhere to be seen.*

MRS YANG (*to the priest, who is pointing to his watch*). Don't be in such a hurry. It can only be a matter of a few minutes. People are drinking and smoking, and no one is in a rush.

She sits down among the guests.

SHEN TE. But shouldn't we talk about how we will manage later?

MRS YANG. Oh please, not a word about business today! It does so cheapen a celebration.

The doorbell rings. All look in the direction of the door, but no one enters.

SHEN TE. Who is your mother expecting, Sun?

YANG SUN. Let that be a surprise for you. By the way, what's your cousin Shui Ta up to? I got on well with him. A sensible chap! Smart! Why don't you say anything?

SHEN TE. I don't know. I don't want to think about him.

YANG SUN. Why ever not?

SHEN TE. Because you shouldn't get on with him. If you love me, you can't love him.

YANG SUN. Then may the three devils of fog, fuel shortage and mechanical failure take him! Drink, you stubborn thing! (*He makes her.*)

THE SISTER-IN-LAW (*to* MRS SHIN). There's something amiss here.

SHIN. What did you expect?

PRIEST (*stepping resolutely up to* MRS YANG, *with his watch in hand*). I have to go, Mrs Yang. I've got another wedding to go to, and a funeral in the morning.

MRS YANG. Do you think I'm happy to have everything get so behindhand? We were hoping to get by with just one pitcher of wine. See, it's almost finished now. (*Aloud to* SHEN TE.) My dear Shen Te, I don't understand what's keeping your cousin!

SHEN TE. My cousin?

MRS YANG. It's him we're waiting for, precious. I'm sufficiently old-fashioned to think that such a close relative of the bride's should be present at the wedding.

SHEN TE. Oh Sun, is it because of the two hundred dollars?

YANG SUN (*not looking at her*). She told you why. She's old-fashioned. I respect that. We'll leave it for another fifteen minutes, and then, if the three devils really have got hold of him, then we'll start!

MRS YANG. You must all have heard that my son is getting a job as a mail pilot. I'm very pleased for him. It's important to earn a large salary nowadays.

THE SISTER-IN-LAW. That's in Peking, isn't it?

MRS YANG. Yes, in Peking.

SHEN TE. Sun, you must tell your mother that Peking's off.

YANG SUN. Your cousin can tell her, if that's what he thinks. Between you and me I think differently.

SHEN TE (*in alarm*). Sun!

YANG SUN. How I loathe this Sichuan! What a dump! Do you want to know how they all look to me, when I half-close my eyes? Horses. They turn their heads in apprehension: what's that roaring past them in the air? Hello, they're outmoded? What's that, their time is up? Let them bite each other to death in their horse town! God I want to get away from here!

SHEN TE. I told you I can't raise the extra two hundred.

YANG SUN. Yes, you did. So it's as well your cousin's coming. Now drink up and leave the business to us! We'll sort it out.

SHEN TE (*appalled*). But my cousin can't come!

YANG SUN. What do you mean?

SHEN TE. He's not around any more.

YANG SUN. So what's our future, can you tell me that?

SHEN TE. I thought you'd still got the three hundred silver dollars. We could buy back the tobacco, which is worth much more, and sell it to the cement workers.

YANG SUN. Forget it! Forget it in a hurry, sister! I'm to stand on the pavement and flog tobacco to cement workers? I, Yang Sun the airman! Frankly, I'd rather blow the three hundred in one night. I'd rather chuck it in the river than do that! And your cousin knows me. I arranged that he would bring the other two hundred along to the wedding.

SHEN TE. My cousin cannot come.

YANG SUN. And I was thinking he couldn't stay away.

SHEN TE. He cannot be where I am.

YANG SUN. How mysterious!

SHEN TE. He is no friend of yours, Sun, you must understand that.

It's me that loves you. My cousin Shui Ta loves no one. he's my friend, but no friend of any of my other friends. He agreed that you should have the three hundred silver dollars, because he was thinking of the pilot's job in Peking. But he won't bring the two hundred to our wedding.

YANG SUN. And why not?

SHEN TE (*looking into his eyes*). He said you only bought one ticket to Peking.

YANG SUN. That may have been the case yesterday, but look what I've got for you today. (*He pulls two pieces of paper halfway out of his breast pocket.*) The old woman doesn't need to see those. They're two tickets to Peking, for you and me. Do you still think your cousin's opposed to our wedding?

SHEN TE. No, it's a good job. And I don't have the shop any more.

YANG SUN. I sold the furniture for your sake.

SHEN TE. Don't say any more! Don't show me the tickets! I'm too afraid I might simply go off with you. Sun, I can't give you the two hundred silver dollars.

YANG SUN. What am I going to do? (*Pause.*) Have a drink! Or are you one of those cautious types? I hate cautious women. When I drink, I feel I'll fly again. And if you drink, you'll understand me, maybe.

SHEN TE. Don't think I don't understand you. You want to fly and I can't help you.

YANG SUN. 'Here's an airplane for you, love, sorry it's just got one wing!'

SHEN TE. Sun, we're not able to come by the Peking job honestly. So I need the three hundred silver dollars back from you. Give them to me now, Sun!

YANG SUN. 'Give them to me now, Sun!' What are you talking about anyway? Are you my wife or aren't you? You're betraying me, you know that? Luckily for you, it's not up to you any more, because everything's been fixed.

MRS YANG (*icily*). Sun, are you sure the bride's cousin will be coming? His absence seems to suggest this wedding doesn't meet with his approval.

YANG SUN. Mum, honestly! He and I are completely together in this. I'll push the door ajar so that he sees us the moment he arrives to give the bride away to his old pal Sun.

He goes over to the door and pushes it open with his foot. Then, swaying a little, having drunk too much, he returns and sits by SHEN TE.

Let's wait. Your cousin has more sense than you do. Love, he wisely observes, is a part of life. And, more important, he knows what that would mean to you, no shop any more and no wedding!

They wait.

MRS YANG. Now!

Footsteps are heard, and all eyes are on the door. But the steps go past.

MRS SHIN. There's a scandal. I can feel it. I can smell it. The bride is waiting for the wedding, but the groom is waiting for the bride's cousin.

YANG SUN. The bride's cousin is taking his time.

SHEN TE (*quietly*). Oh Sun!

YANG SUN. Having to sit here with the tickets in my pocket, next to a ninny who can't do simple addition! I can see the day coming when you'll set the police on me to recover your three hundred silver dollars.

SHEN TE (*to the audience*). He's a bad man, and he wants me to be bad as well. Here I am, I love him, and he's waiting for my cousin. But seated around me are the poor and the helpless, the people who wait at my door in the morning for rice, and an unknown man in Peking who's afraid for his job. And they all protect me, by putting their trust in me.

YANG SUN (*staring at the glass pitcher, where the wine is all but gone*). The glass pitcher of wine is our clock. We are poor folk, and when the guests have drunk it all, our time is up.

MRS YANG motions him to be quiet, as further footsteps are heard.

WAITER (*entering*). Another pitcher of wine, Mrs Yang?

MRS YANG. No, I think we've had enough. Wine only makes you warm after all.

MRS SHIN. I expect it costs money too.

MRS YANG. Drinking always makes me sweat.

WAITER. I must ask you to settle your bill then please.

MRS YANG (*ignoring him*). I appeal to everyone to be patient just a little longer, the relative must be on his way. (*To the WAITER.*) Don't disturb the celebrations!

WAITER. I can't let you leave unless you settle the bill.

MRS YANG. But everyone knows me here!

WAITER. Precisely!

MRS YANG. The service nowadays is unbelievable! What do you say, Sun?

PRIEST. I'm off (*Exits importantly.*)

MRS YANG (*desperately*). Please everyone remain seated! The priest will be back in a few minutes.

YANG SUN. Oh, forget it, mum. Ladies and gentlemen, seeing as the priest's gone, we won't detain you any longer.

THE SISTER-IN-LAW. Come on, grandpa!

THE GRANDFATHER (*earnestly emptying his glass*). To the bride!

THE NIECE (*to SHEN TE*). Don't take it amiss. He means well. He's fond of you.

MRS SHIN. That's what I call a debacle!

All the guests exeunt.

SHEN TE. Shall I go too, Sun?

YANG SUN. No, you stay. (*He pulls at her dress, so it goes all askew*.) Isn't it your wedding? I'm still waiting, and my old woman's waiting too. She wants to see her falcon take to the air. But, quite honestly, pigs will have wings before she ever steps outside and sees me flying over her home. (*To the empty chairs, as if the guests were still there*.) Talk amongst yourselves, ladies and gentlemen! Don't you like it here? The wedding's just been put back a little, on account of the important relative who's expected, and because the bride doesn't understand the meaning of love. To entertain you, the bridegroom, which is me, will now sing you a song.

YANG SUN *sings:* Pigs Will Fly

The story goes, and it's generally known,
That the poor boy will one day sit on a golden throne.
Pigs will fly,
And he'll be sitting on a golden throne.

Crime won't pay, and virtue will carry a guarantee,
The going rate for a job will be mutually agreed.
Pigs will fly,
And wages will be mutually agreed.

And the grass'll touch the sky, and pebbles flow upstream,
Man will be good, and the earth a pleasant dream.
Pigs will fly,
And the earth will be a pleasant dream.

And then I'll be a pilot, and you'll be top brass,
She'll get a holiday, and you will get a job at last.
Pigs will fly,
And you will get a job at last.

And because our patience is all but gone,
All this is gonna come to pass just at the crack of dawn.
Pigs will fly, pigs will fly,
In close formation at the crack of dawn.

MRS YANG. He won't come now.

The three of them sit there and two of them are looking towards the door.

Interlude

WANG's *Sleeping Place.*

Once more the water-seller sees the gods in a dream. He's fallen asleep over a large book. Music.

WANG. Thank goodness you've come, Enlightened Ones! There is
a question which has been preoccupying me. In the derelict
hut of a former priest who has gone to work in the cement
factory, I found a book which contains this remarkable
passage. I have to read it to you. This is it.

*With his left hand he leafs through an imaginary book on top of
the actual one that's lying in his lap, and he raises this imaginary
book to read from it, while the actual one is left lying on his lap.*

'In Sung there is a village called the Orchard of Thorns.
Catalpas, cypresses and mulberry trees grow there. Those trees
that measure a span or two in circumference are cut down by
people requiring bars for their dog kennels. Those that are
three or four feet in circumference are cut down by rich and
distinguished families requiring planks for coffins. Those that
measure seven or eight feet in circumference are cut down by
those looking for beams for their luxury villas. In this way,
none of the trees reach the term of their natural life, but all
are cut down by the axe and the saw. This is the curse of
usefulness.'

THIRD GOD. But that would mean the most useless person would
be the best.

WANG. No, not the best, but the most fortunate. The least good
is the most fortunate.

FIRST GOD. The things people write!

SECOND GOD. What is it about this parable, water-seller, that so
agitates you?

WANG. I'm thinking of Shen Te, Enlightened One. Her love has
foundered for want of ruthlessness. Is it possible that she is
too good for this world, O Enlightened Ones!

FIRST GOD. Nonsense, you weak and miserable man! It would

appear you have been consumed by your lice and your doubts.

WANG. Assuredly, Enlightened One! Forgive me! I just thought you might be able to do something.

FIRST GOD. Out of the question. Yesterday our friend here (*Pointing to the* THIRD GOD, *who is sporting a black eye.*) intervened in a quarrel, and you see what happened to him.

WANG. But the cousin has had to be summoned again. I have seen for myself what an exceptionally able man he is, but even he couldn't do anything. It looks as though the shop is lost.

THIRD GOD (*concerned*). Perhaps we should help after all?

FIRST GOD. I am of the opinion that she should help herself.

SECOND GOD (*severely*). The worse the situation, the better the good person performs in it. Suffering is a great purgative!

FIRST GOD. We're pinning all our hopes on her now.

THIRD GOD. Our search hasn't been terribly successful to date. We find the odd attempt to be virtuous, some commendable resolutions, many noble principles, but none of them make a good person. Wherever we've met anyone who was halfway good, they were living in degrading conditions. (*Confidingly.*) We've been experiencing particular difficulty over accommodation. You can tell we've been roughing it by all these straws that are sticking to us.

WANG. Just one thing. Couldn't you at least . . .

THE GODS. Nothing. – We have only observer status. – We firmly believe our good person will make her way on this dark earth. – Her strength will increase with each new burden she takes up. – You will see, water-seller, that everything will turn out . . .

The shapes of the gods have become paler all the time, and their voices fainter. Now they disappear entirely, and their voices are silent.

Scene Six

The Yard Behind Shen Te's Tobacco Shop

A few household things in a cart. SHEN TE *and* MRS SHIN *are taking laundry down from a clothesline.*

MRS SHIN. You see, now you've lost your shop, and everybody knows your airman is drinking away the money in the lowest bars. (SHEN TE *doesn't reply.*)

It's all gone. No man, no tobacco, no place to live. That's what you get for wanting to be a cut above the rest of us. Now what are you going to live off?

SHEN TE. I don't know. Perhaps I can earn some money by sorting tobacco. (*A child appears in the gate of the yard.*)

MRS SHIN (*shooing it away*). Get lost you! (*To* SHEN TE.) These street-vultures only have to sniff a foreclosure and there they are, hoping to fill their pockets.

SHEN TE. Let him pick over the rubbish. Maybe he'll find something he can use.

MRS SHIN. If there's anything usable in there, I'm having it. You haven't paid me for the laundry yet. Go away, or I'll call the police. (*The child disappears.*)

SHEN TE. Why are you so angry?

> *To the audience.*
> Is it not fatiguing
> To lash out at one's fellow creatures?
> Greed causes the veins in the temple to swell.
> Naturally extended, one's hand is equally ready
> To give and to receive. Only to snatch greedily
> Requires an effort. The seductiveness of charity!
> How pleasant it is to be amiable!
> A kind word slips out
> Like a sigh of contentment.

MRS SHIN. You should tell that to your cousin some time. By the way, what are Mr Shui Ta's trousers doing here? He must have left here naked.

SHEN TE. He has another pair.

MRS SHIN. I thought you said he'd gone for good? Why then, has he left his trousers behind?

SHEN TE. He won't need them any more.

MRS SHIN. So you don't want to take them?

SHEN TE. No.

THE CARPENTER, *Lin To, appears in the gateway.*

THE CARPENTER. Good day, Miss Shen Te. There is a rumour going round the area that you've secured shelter for the homeless in the houses belonging to the barber Shu Fu. Is that true?

MRS SHIN. It was true. But as we've subsequently jilted Mr Shu Fu, your shelter's gone for a burton.

THE CARPENTER. That's a pity. I don't know where I can go now with my family.

MRS SHIN. Miss Shen Te will shortly be in the happy position of having to ask *you* for shelter. (*Exit* THE CARPENTER, *disappointed*.) There'll be several more coming like him.

SHEN TE. That's awful.

MRS SHIN. As you're too good for the barber, the typhoid huts by the river will just have to do for the likes of Lin To and his family. I do believe you're still stuck on your pilot, however badly he treated you. Doesn't it matter to you that he's such a bad person?

SHEN TE. But it's only because of poverty.

To the audience.
I saw him puff out his cheeks in sleep: they were evil.
And in the morning I held his jacket up against the light,
And I could see the wall through it.
When I saw his duplicitous smile, I was frightened, but
When I saw the holes in his shoes, I loved him very much.

MRS SHIN. So you're defending him too? I've never come across anything so perverse. (*Angry*.) It will be a relief to get you out of here.

SHEN TE (*reels as she takes down the washing*). I feel a bit dizzy.

SHIN (*takes the clothes from her*). Do you feel dizzy when you stretch or bend? I expect you're pregnant! Your pilot's played a fine trick on you! He's left you with a bun in the oven!

She goes backstage with the laundry basket. SHEN TE *watches her go without moving. Then she looks at her belly, touches it and a great joy appears on her face.*

SHEN TE (*quietly*). Oh joy! There is a small person being born inside me. You can't see anything yet. But I know he's there. The world is waiting for him, secretly. In the cities they are saying: there is a man coming who will be someone to reckon with.

(*She presents her little son to the audience.*)
An airman!
Greet the new conqueror
Of uncharted regions and inaccessible mountain chains. A man
Who carries the mail over inhospitable deserts
From one person to another!

She starts walking to and fro, leading her son by the hand.
Come, my son. Take a look at the world. This here is a tree. Bow and greet it. (*She shows him how.*) There, now you're acquainted. Stop, here comes the water-seller. He is a friend, you may shake his hand. Don't be afraid! A glass of fresh water for my son. It's a warm day. (*She gives him the glass.*) Uh oh, the policeman! We'll avoid him. Perhaps we'll treat ourselves to a few cherries from the garden of the rich Mr Feh Pung. But we mustn't let him see us! Come on, little fatherless one! You want cherries just the same! Quietly, son, quietly! (*They go on tiptoe, circumspectly.*) No, this way, we can hide behind that bush. No, it's a mistake to go straight up to it, in this case. (*He appears to be pulling her one way, she to resist.*) We must be sensible. (*Suddenly she gives in.*) All right, if you want to head directly for it . . . (*She lifts him up.*) Can you reach the cherries? Stuff them in your mouth, that's the best hiding place for them. (*She eats one herself, which he puts in her mouth.*) Mmm, sweet. Drat it, here's the policeman. Now we have to run. (*They flee.*) There's the street. Easy now, just walk along normally, so we don't catch his eye. As if nothing had

happened at all . . . (*She sings, strolling with the child.*)

A plum fell out of the sky
And attacked a passer-by.
The fellow stopped
And watched it drop
And into his mouth it popped.

The child has reappeared in the gateway. It watches SHEN TE's *game in amazement. All at once, she sees it and beckons to it to come into the yard.*

NI TZU. Where are you going to go?

SHEN TE. I don't know, Ni Tzu.

The child rubs its belly and looks at her hopefully.

I have no more rice left, Ni Tzu, not a grain.

NI TZU. Stay.

SHEN TE. I'd like to.

The cries of the water-seller, 'Buy Water', are heard.

NI TZU. Thirsty.

SHEN TE. That's something I can get for you. Wait here, little man!

She runs to the gate, where the water-seller has appeared.

WANG. Good day, Shen Te. Is it true you're having to leave your shop?

SHEN TE. That doesn't matter. I feel happy. I'm having a child, Wang. I'm glad you're here. I had to tell someone. Only don't tell anyone else about it otherwise Yang Sun will get to hear, and he doesn't want us. Give me a cupful.

He gives her a cupful of water. When she turns round with it, she sees the child and freezes. It's gone across to the dustbin and is rummaging around in it, picks out something and eats it.

SHEN TE (*to the water-seller*). Go away, I don't feel well. (*She pushes him away.*) It's hungry. It's rummaging around in the dustbin.

She picks up the child and in a great speech she expresses her horror over the lot of poor children, showing the audience its little grey face. She is quite determined that her own child will never be treated so mercilessly. While she speaks, the music for The Song of the Defencelessness of the Gods and the Good *begins.*

O my son! My airman! What a world
Will you be born into? They want to have you
Scavenge in dustbins, you too!
See his little grey face!
(*She shows the child off.*) Is this
The way you treat your own kind?
Have you no compassion for the fruit
Of your womb? No compassion
For yourselves, unhappy people?
I will defend my child, if I have to
Become a tigress. Yes, from this hour
When I have seen this, I will cut myself off
From everyone and not rest
Until I have saved my own son at least!
All I have learned in the gutter,
The viciousness and the deceit, will be
For you. Son, I will
Be good to you, and to all others be a tigress
And a wild beast, if I must. And I must.

Interlude

The water-seller comes walking along the front of the stage in front of the curtain, as if it were a street. He stops and addresses the audience.

WANG. Can you tell me, ladies and gentlemen, where Miss Shen Te from Sandalmakers' Lane can have got to? For the last seven months she's completely vanished. Her cousin suddenly appeared, for the third time, and strange business has been transacted in the tobacco shop, very profitable but unscrupulous business. (*Quietly.*) Opium. – The worst of it is that I've lost contact with the three Enlightened Ones. Perhaps it's because I'm so upset that I can't sleep, and so I've stopped having dreams. Anyway, if you should happen to see Shen Te, tell her we're anxious to hear news of her; we miss her very much in the area, she was such a good person. (*He goes sadly on his way.*)

Scene Seven

Shen Te's Tobacco Shop

The shop has become an office with deep armchairs and thick carpets. SHUI TA *expensively dressed, and fat, is seeing off* THE HUSBAND *and* THE WIFE *and* THE NEPHEW *who once visited* SHEN TE *on the day the shop opened.* MRS SHIN, *wearing strikingly new clothing, looks on in amusement. It is raining outside.*

SHUI TA. For the umpteenth time, I never saw any sacks in the back room.

THE WIFE. In that case we'd like to write to Miss Shen Te. What is her address?

SHUI TA. I'm afraid I can't help you.

THE NEPHEW. I see. The sacks have gone but you've grown rich.

SHUI TA. So it would appear.

MRS SHIN. You should really let the matter rest. After all, Mr Shui Ta has given your family work in his tobacco factory. His patience has limits.

THE WIFE. But the work is damaging the boy's health.

SHUI TA *and* MRS SHIN *remain silent.*

THE HUSBAND. Let's go, we have no proof about the sacks. But maybe Shen Te will come back one day.

SHUI TA *shrugs his shoulders.* THE HUSBAND *and* THE WIFE *leave crossly with* THE NEPHEW.

SHUI TA (*weakly*). The work in the tobacco factory is damaging his health! Work is work.

MRS SHIN. Those two mingy sacks wouldn't have got those people very far. That kind of thing is just useful seed capital. To develop it into actual wealth requires talents of a very high order. That's where you come in.

SHUI TA (*who has to sit down, as he feels sick*). I feel dizzy again.

MRS SHIN (*tending to him*). You're in your seventh month. These excitements are bad for you. You're lucky you've got me. Everybody has to have some help from somewhere. I'll stand by you in your time of need. (*She laughs.*)

SHUI TA (*weakly*). May I count on that, Mrs Shin?

MRS SHIN. Of course you can! It'll cost you though.

A man in stylish clothes comes in. It's THE UNEMPLOYED MAN, *who was given cigarettes on the day the shop opened.*

AGENT. The accounts, Mr Shui Ta. Sales to street customers to the tune of fifty silver dollars. Sales at the Teahouse of Felicity . . .

SHUI TA (*with difficulty*). Go please. Tomorrow.

MRS SHIN. Can't you see that Mr Shui Ta is poorly?

AGENT. We have a problem with the police in the fourth district. A consignment has got into the wrong hands, Mr Shui Ta.

MRS SHIN. Are you incapable of managing anything on your own? (*The frightened* AGENT *makes to leave.*)

SHUI TA. Hold it! Money!

The AGENT *hands over money and goes.*

MRS SHIN. Loosen your collar, and you'll feel better.

SHUI TA (*miserably*). It's all for the sake of the child, Mrs Shin.

MRS SHIN. All for the child.

SHUI TA. I'm getting such a fat belly. That must attract notice.

MRS SHIN. People put it down to wealth.

SHUI TA. What's going to become of the little one?

MRS SHIN. You ask me that three times a day. It'll be looked after, the best care that money can buy.

SHUI TA. Yes. (*Apprehensively.*) And it must never see Shui Ta.

MRS SHIN. Never. Only Shen Te.

SHUI TA. The gossip on the streets! The water-seller and his speeches! The snooping round the shop!

MRS SHIN. Have a drink of water. (*She fetches water.*) Why don't you get out of here, and move to a villa in a good part of town? But I know the answer to that. You're hoping that degenerate pilot will turn up. Weakness.

SHUI TA. That's not true.

A ragged person comes in through the door, the former airman YANG SUN. *He's surprised to find* SHUI TA *in the arms of* MRS SHIN, *who's just giving him water.*

YANG SUN (*thickly*). Am I interrupting?

SHUI TA *gets up cumbersomely and stares at him.*

MRS SHIN. Mr Yang Sun in person!

YANG SUN (*submissively*). Excuse my coming to visit you in this garb, Mr Shui Ta. I've been separated from my luggage, and I refused to let the rain prevent me from looking up an old acquaintance, you understand.

SHUI TA (*takes* MRS SHIN *aside, before she can say anything*). Go and find him some clothes.

MRS SHIN. You should throw him out right now. I'm warning you.

SHUI TA (*sharply*). Do what I tell you. (*Exit* MRS SHIN, *reluctantly.*)

YANG SUN. Thick carpets! That's money. I've heard they call you the Tobacco King now, Mr Shui Ta!

SHUI TA. I've been fortunate.

YANG SUN. Oh, come on, Mr Shui Ta, it's not just good fortune, it's merit. Yes, some grow fat and others thin, hey?

SHUI TA. I may take it adverse circumstances have dogged you, Mr Yang Sun, but are you ill?

YANG SUN. Me? No, I'm in good health.

SHUI TA. I'm glad to hear it. It would seem that ruined health is one thing that cannot be repaired.

MRS SHIN *returns from the back room with clothing.*

I hope these things fit you. Is the hat a bit big?

MRS SHIN *puts the hat on* YANG SUN's *head.*

Yes, it's too big. Get another, Mrs Shin.

YANG SUN. I don't want a hat. (*Suddenly angry.*) What are you playing at? Fobbing me off with an old hat! (*Masters himself.*) What do I want with your hat? I need something else. (*Crawling.*) Mr Shui Ta, will you make an unhappy man's single wish come true?

SHUI TA. How can I help you?

MRS SHIN. Isn't it obvious? I'll tell you what he wants!

SHUI TA (*dawning on him*). No!

MRS SHIN. Opium, eh?

SHUI TA. Sun!

YANG SUN. Just a little bag, two or three pipes! That's all I'm asking for. I'm not bothered about clothes or food, but I have to have my pipes.

SHUI TA (*aghast*). Not opium! Don't tell me you've fallen victim to that scourge! You must know that the unhappy souls who use it to escape their misery for an hour or two, are delivered into such lasting misery that they soon use the poison not to achieve bliss, but to diminish extremes of suffering.

YANG SUN. I see you're well-informed: that about describes my condition.

SHUI TA. Turn back! Overcome your addiction, don't touch the poison again, I'm sure you can do it.

YANG SUN. That's what you say, Mr Shui Ta, who deal in it and understand everything! But your livelihood depends on us smokers not finding the way back.

SHUI TA. Water! I feel sick.

MRS SHIN (*tending to him*). You haven't been yourself of late, not the man you used to be. (*Sarcastically.*) But perhaps it's the rain which has accompanied Mr Yang Sun. Rain always seems to make you irritable and melancholy, why, I'm sure I have no idea.

SHUI TA. Get out!

Voice of the water-seller singing:

WANG. I sell water for a living –
And now it's pissing down like hell.
Had to walk for miles this morning
To fill this bucket at the well.
      Water!
Thirsty and parched,
No one will try it,
No one pays me,
And no one buys it.
(Buy water, you bastards!)

MRS SHIN. It's that damned water-seller. He'll be launching into one of his tirades again soon. (*Exit, on a gesture from* SHUI TA.)

WANG'S VOICE. Is there no good person left in the city? Not even here, where the good Shen Te used to live? Where is she, who bought a cup of my water even when it was raining, many months ago, in the abundance of her heart? Where is she now? Has no one seen her? Has no one heard from her? She went into this house one evening, and has never been seen since.

YANG SUN (*urgently*). Let's make a deal: give me what I want, and I'll gag him for you.

WANG (*enters*). Mr Shui Ta, I'm asking you once more when Shen Te will return. Seven months have passed since she went on her travels. (SHUI TA *remains silent.*) There have been goings-on here which she would never have countenanced. (SHUI TA *still silent.*) Mr Shui Ta, I've heard rumours that something has happened to Shen Te. We, her friends, are deeply concerned. Be so good as to tell us her address!

SHUI TA. I'm sorry, Mr Wang, I have no time just now. Come

back next week.

WANG (*more agitated*). It has been commented upon that the rice which always used to be given to the hungry here, has been on the doorstep again of late.

SHUI TA. What do you infer from that?

WANG. That Shen Te has not gone away at all.

SHUI TA. No? (WANG *remains silent*.) Then I'll give you my reply. It's final. If you are Shen Te's friend, Mr Wang, then you should cease to ask after her. That's my advice to you.

WANG. Fine advice! Mr Shui Ta, Shen Te told me before she disappeared that she was pregnant.

YANG SUN. What's that?

SHUI TA (*quickly*). That's a lie!

WANG (*very earnestly to* SHUI TA). Mr Shui Ta, don't think that Shen Te's friends will ever cease to ask after her. A good person is not so easily forgotten. There are very few. (*Exit*.)

Motionless, SHUI TA *watches him go. Then he hurries into the back room.*

YANG SUN (*to the audience, transformed*). Shen Te's pregnant! This is outrageous! I have been duped! She must have told her cousin and that rotter must have sent her away at once. 'Pack your bags and clear out before the child's father gets to hear of it!' It's completely unnatural. Inhuman. I have a son. A new Yang is on the scene! And what happens? The girl vanishes and I'm allowed to become so dissipated that that wretched water-seller doesn't even recognise me! (*He is furious*.) I'm fobbed off with an old hat! (*He tramples on it*.) Criminal! Robber! Kidnapper! The girl's effectively without a protector! (*A sob is audible from the back room. He stands still*.) Wasn't that sobbing? Who is it? It's stopped. What's that sobbing in the back room? That hard bastard Shui Ta wouldn't sob! So who's that sobbing? And what's the significance of the rice on the doorstep in the morning? Is the girl still here? Is he just hiding her? Who else would be in there sobbing? That would be a gift from the gods! If she's pregnant, I've got to get hold of her!

SHUI TA *returns from the back room. He walks over to the door and looks out at the rain.*

YANG SUN. So where is she?

SHUI TA (*raises his hand and listens*). One moment! It's nine o'clock! But you won't hear anything today. It's raining too hard.

YANG SUN. What are you listening for?

SHUI TA. The mail plane.

YANG SUN. Don't give me that.

SHUI TA. I seem to remember you once wanting to fly. Does flying no longer interest you?

YANG SUN (*cautiously*). Why do you ask? Do you want to fix me up with a job as a pilot? Now? Do you think I can fly a plane with these hands? (*He holds them up. They are shaking.*) Where's my fiancée? Listen, I'm asking you, where's my fiancée Shen Te?

SHUI TA. Do you really want to know?

YANG SUN. You betcha!

SHUI TA. That might be of interest to my cousin.

YANG SUN. I am sufficiently concerned for her that I wouldn't be inclined to overlook it if she had been deprived of her liberty, say.

SHUI TA. By whom?

YANG SUN. By you.

Pause.

SHUI TA. What would you do in such an eventuality?

YANG SUN (*roughly*). I would urge you to supply me with what I want, and no more backchat.

SHUI TA. Supply you with . . .

YANG SUN (*thickly*). With the dope of course.

SHUI TA. I see. (*Pause.*) Mr Yang Sun, I will never let you have so much as a pinch of that poison.

YANG SUN. But perhaps your cousin wouldn't refuse the father of her child a couple of pipes of opium a day, and a bench to sleep on? Brother-in-law, my desire for the queen of my heart is unquenchable. I feel I have to do something to get her back in my arms. (*He shouts.*) Shen Te! Shen Te!

SHUI TA. Haven't you heard that Shen Te has gone travelling? You may inspect the back room if you like.

YANG SUN (*giving him a peculiar look*). No, I wouldn't, or at least not on my own. I'm not in physical shape for a punch-up with you. The police, it seems to me, are better fed.

He exits quickly, taking care not to turn his back on SHUI TA.

Impassively SHUI TA watches him leave. Then he goes quickly into the back room and takes out various things of SHEN TE's; linen, toilet articles, a dress. He looks long at the scarf YANG SUN praised in the park. Then he makes a parcel of them. Then he gets a suitcase and some men's clothes, and packs them.

SHUI TA (*with bundle and suitcase*). So this is it. After so much effort and so much success, I have to abandon my flourishing business, which I built up from this poky little shop, which the gods thought was sufficient. A single weakness, an unpredictable attack of indulgence, plunges me into the abyss. The moment I allowed this dissolute man to open his mouth instead of handing him over to the police, for embezzlement of three hundred dollars, I was ruined. No amount of toughness, of inhumanity, is enough, if it isn't absolute. Such is the world.

Hearing sounds outside, he quickly shoves the bundle under the table. A stone is thrown through the window. Voices of agitated people outside. Enter YANG SUN, WANG and THE POLICEMAN.

THE POLICEMAN. Mr Shui Ta, it is much to our regret that the agitated mood of the quarter compels us to pursue a charge that your cousin, Miss Shen Te, has been deprived of her liberty by you.

SHUI TA. That isn't true.

THE POLICEMAN. Mr Yang Sun assures me that he heard sobbing coming from the room behind your office, sobbing which could only have been produced by a woman.

YANG SUN (*points to the suitcase*). He's packed and ready. He was about to make a run for it!

THE POLICEMAN. I'm afraid it's my duty to inspect the room in question, Mr Shui Ta.

SHUI TA *opens the door*. THE POLICEMAN *steps inside, bowing on the threshold. He looks inside, turns round and smiles.*

There is no one here.

YANG SUN (*who has stepped in with him*). But I heard sobbing! (*His eyes light on the table under which* SHUI TA *has stuffed his bundle. He runs across to it.*) That wasn't there just now!

Opening it, he holds out SHEN TE's *clothes, etc.*

WANG. These are Shen Te's things! (*He runs over to the door and shouts out.*) Her clothes have been found!

THE POLICEMAN (*taking possession of the items*). You say that your cousin has gone away. A bundle of her personal effects is found under the table. Where is the girl contactable, Mr Shui Ta?

SHUI TA. I have no address for her.

THE POLICEMAN. That is most unfortunate.

CALLS FROM THE CROWD OUTSIDE. Shen Te's things have been found! The Tobacco King has murdered her and hidden the body!

THE POLICEMAN. Mr Shui Ta, I must ask you to accompany me to the station.

SHUI TA *merely bows and precedes* THE POLICEMAN *out.*

WANG. An appalling crime has taken place!

YANG SUN (*dismayed*). But I heard sobbing!

Interlude

Wang's Sleeping Place

Music. For the last time, the gods appear in the dreams of the water-seller. They are greatly changed. They bear the unmistakeable signs of long wandering, deep exhaustion and numerous unpleasant experiences. One has had the hat knocked off his head. Another has had his foot caught in a foxtrap, and all three are barefooted.

WANG. There you are at last! Terrible things are happening in Shen Te's tobacco shop, O Enlightened Ones! Shen Te has been gone for months now! The cousin has taken over! Today he was arrested. They say he has murdered her, to get control of the shop. But I don't believe that, because I had a dream in which she appeared before me and told me her cousin was holding her prisoner. Oh, Enlightened Ones, you must come quickly and find her.

FIRST GOD. That's dreadful. Our whole quest has been a failure. We found few good people, and those we did find were leading lives that were not fit for human beings. We had decided to pin our hopes on Shen Te.

SECOND GOD. If only she's still good!

WANG. She surely is, but she's disappeared!

FIRST GOD. Then all is lost.

SECOND GOD. Buck up!

FIRST GOD. What's the use? We'll have to abdicate if we don't find her! What a world has presented itself to our eyes! Misery, meanness and rubbish everywhere! Even the landscape has declined. The trees have been topped by pylons, and beyond the mountains we have seen smoke and heard gunfire and nowhere a good person succeeding!

THIRD GOD. Oh, water-seller, our precepts appear to be deadly!

I fear all the moral principles we have established must be scrubbed. People have enough trouble merely to survive. Good intentions take them to the edge of the precipice, good deeds plunge them to their destruction. (*To the other two gods.*) The world is unliveable, you must agree!

SECOND GOD (*vehemently*). No, it's the people who are worthless!

THIRD GOD. Because the world is too harsh!

SECOND GOD. Because people are too weak!

FIRST GOD. Decorum, my friends please! Brothers, we must not despair. We did find one person who was good, and she hasn't turned to the bad, she's merely disappeared. Let's hurry up and find her! One person's enough. Didn't we say that everything may still turn out well if only we can find one person who can endure the world, just one person!

They hurry off.

Scene Eight

Courtroom

In individual groups: the barber SHU FU and the tobacco dealer MI TSU. SHIN and SHUI TA's AGENT (formerly THE UNEMPLOYED MAN), together with THE POLICEMAN. WANG with the family of eight, THE CARPENTER Lin To and the young girl from the Teahouse of Felicity and her mother. YANG SUN alone.

THE HUSBAND. He is too powerful.

WANG. I have assembled as many witnesses as I could.

THE CARPENTER. How can the judge pronounce a just verdict when the friends of the accused, the barber Shu Fu and the tobacco dealer Mi Tsu are his friends also?

THE SISTER-IN-LAW. Yesterday Mrs Shin was observed taking a fat goose to the judge's kitchen, on the instruction of Shui Ta. The fat was dripping through the basket.

THE NIECE. They will never find poor Shen Te.

WANG. Yes, only the gods could get at the truth.

THE POLICEMAN. Silence in court.

Enter the three gods in judicial robes. As they proceed along the edge of the stage to their judicial chairs, one can hear them talking quietly.

THIRD GOD. We'll be found out; our certificates have been so badly forged.

SECOND GOD. And people will be suspicious when they hear of the sudden stomach upset of the judge.

FIRST GOD. No, that had natural causes. He polished off half a goose.

MRS SHIN (*in alarm*). These are new judges!

WANG. And very good ones!

The THIRD GOD, last in the procession, hears this and smiles at WANG. The gods sit down. The FIRST GOD taps his gavel on the table. THE POLICEMAN has gone to fetch SHUI TA, who is received with whistles, but still makes a majestic entrance.

THE POLICEMAN (*chiefly to SHUI TA*). I'm afraid there's a disagreeable surprise for you. The judge is not Fu Yi Cheng. But these new judges look very clement too.

SHUI TA looks at the judges and faints.

THE NIECE. Look, the Tobacco King has fainted!

THE SISTER-IN-LAW. Yes, on seeing the new judges!

WANG. He seems to know them! Now that I don't understand.

FIRST GOD. Are you the tobacco wholesale merchant, Shui Ta?

SHUI TA (*very feebly*). Yes.

FIRST GOD. You have been accused of removing your cousin, Miss Shen Te, in order to take over her shop. How do you plead?

SHUI TA. Not guilty.

FIRST GOD (*leafing through the file*). We'll begin by hearing evidence from the local constable on the respective reputations of the accused and his cousin.

THE POLICEMAN (*steps forward*). Shen Te was a girl who liked to be popular with everybody, who, as they say, lived and let live. Shui Ta on the other hand, is a man of principle. The girl's kindheartedness occasionally forced him to adopt strong measures. But, unlike the girl, he always stayed on the right side of the law, your Honour. I know Mr Shui Ta to be a respectable citizen with respect for the law.

FIRST GOD. Are there others here who would like to testify that the accused could not have committed a crime such as the one of which he stands accused?

MR SHU FU *and the tobacco dealer come forward.*

THE POLICEMAN (*whispering to the gods*). Mr Shu Fu, a highly influential gentleman!

SHU FU. Mr Shui Ta is a much respected businessman in Sichuan. He is deputy head of the chamber of commerce and has been put forward as JP for his area.

WANG (*shouting out*). Put forward by you! You're in cahoots with him!

THE POLICEMAN (*whispering*). A bad lot!

MRS MI TSU. As president of the welfare club, I should like to remind the court that Mr Shui Ta gives bread and employment to many people in his tobacco factories. The aforementioned Shen Te, however, had a rather poor reputation.

THE POLICEMAN (*in a whisper*). Mrs Mi Tsu, a close friend of Judge Fu Yi Cheng!

FIRST GOD. Very well, now let us hear whether anyone has less complimentary things to say about the accused.

WANG, *the* CARPENTER *and the family of eight step forward.*

THE POLICEMAN. The scum of the district!

FIRST GOD. So what can you tell us of the general conduct of the accused?

Confused cries: He's ruined us! – He blackmailed me! – He put us on the road to crime! – Exploited the helpless! – Cheated! – Murdered!

FIRST GOD. Accused, how do you reply?

SHUI TA. I've done nothing but secure the survival of my cousin, Your Honour. I only came when there was a danger she might lose her little shop. I had to come three times. I never meant to stay. Circumstances on the last occasion compelled me to. This time has been very difficult for me. My cousin was popular, but I did the dirty work. That's why I'm so disliked.

THE SISTER-IN-LAW. That you are. Take our case, Your Honour. (*To* SHUI TA.) I won't mention the sacks.

SHUI TA. Why not? Why not?

THE SISTER-IN-LAW (*to the gods*). Shen Te put us up, but he had us put into prison.

SHUI TA. You'd stolen cakes!

THE SISTER-IN-LAW. Now he's pretending to care about the baker's cakes! He wanted to have the shop for himself!

SHUI TA. It was a shop, not a dosshouse, you selfish people!

THE SISTER-IN-LAW. But we had nowhere to stay!

SHUI TA. There were too many of you! The lifeboat was on the point of capsizing. I made it seaworthy once more. There wasn't a single day that I didn't put out rice for the poorest inhabitants. My cousin saw her shop as a gift from the gods.

WANG. But you wanted to flog it off.

SHUI TA. Because my cousin wanted to help an airman to fly. I was to raise the necessary money!

WANG. Maybe that's what she wanted, but you had your eye on that well-paid job in Peking. The shop wasn't good enough for you!

SHUI TA. My cousin lacked all business sense!

MRS SHIN. Besides, she was in love with the airman.

SHUI TA. Should she not be allowed to love?

WANG. Of course! So why did *you* try to force her into a marriage with a man she didn't love, the barber here?

SHUI TA. Because the man she did love was no good.

FIRST GOD (*interested*). So whom did she love?

MRS SHIN (*pointing to* YANG SUN, *who's sitting there brutishly*). Him. The proverb says: Birds of a feather flock together. That was the private life of your angel of the suburbs!

WANG (*angrily*). She didn't love him because he was like her, but because he was wretched. She didn't just help him because she loved him; she also loved him because she helped him.

SECOND GOD. You're right. A love like that was not beneath her.

SHUI TA. But it was life-threatening!

FIRST GOD. Wasn't he the one who accused you of murdering her?

YANG SUN. Of kidnapping her. He couldn't have murdered her, because only a few minutes before his arrest, I heard Shen Te's voice from the room at the back of the shop.

FIRST GOD (*avidly*). So she was alive then? Tell us exactly what you heard?

YANG SUN. It was her sobbing, Your Honour.

THIRD GOD. And you were able to recognise that?

YANG SUN. Shouldn't I recognise her voice?

SHU FU. Yes, you drove her to sobbing often enough!

YANG SUN. But still I made her happy. And then he (*Pointing to* SHUI TA.) wanted to sell her to you.

SHUI TA (*to* YANG SUN). Because you didn't love her!

YANG SUN. I didn't have a job.

WANG (*to* SHUI TA). The only thing you cared about was Shu Fu's money.

SHUI TA. But what was the money needed for, Your Honour? (*To* YANG SUN). You wanted her to give up everything for you, but the barber offered his houses and his money to help the poor. If she'd married the barber, it would have enabled her to do more good. But she didn't want to do that.

WANG. So now it's Shen Te's fault that the good wasn't done!

SHUI TA. That's often how it was!

MRS SHIN. All the good she did! Look at the man she tried to help! (*Points to* YANG SUN.) And look (*Pointing to the* AGENT.) at Mr Li Gung, whom Shui Ta has helped. Seven months ago, he walked into the shop, he didn't have any work and he was begging for a cigarette. Now he's got a good job as a Commercial Agent.

AGENT (*standing up*). That's true, Mr Shui Ta has helped me to lead a decent life.

MOTHER OF THE GIRL ADDICT (*gets up, to her daughter*). That's him, isn't it? (*She nods.*) He deals in opium. And now it's been established that he's on Mr Shui Ta's payroll.

WANG. Yes, that's typical of the way you help people, Shui Ta! And Shen Te had to go, so that you could keep your opium business going. Admit that you've been dealing in narcotics!

SHUI TA. It was for the child's sake!

THE WIFE (*livid*). And what about *my* child?

THE CARPENTER. And our children? Shen Te's protégés? You put them to work in your festering factory, O Tobacco King!

SHUI TA *is silent.*

THE GRANDFATHER (*given a signal by* WANG, *steps forward majestically*). The work is unhealthy. The boy has been coughing.

WANG. That shut you up! The gods gave Shen Te her shop to be a little source of good in the world. She was always out to do good, and you kept coming along and preventing her.

SHUI TA (*beside himself*). Because otherwise the source would have dried up, you fool!

MRS SHIN. That's right, Your Honour!

WANG. What use is a source you can't drink from?

SHUI TA. Good deeds are ruinous!

WANG (*livid*). But evil deeds are a good living, ha? What have you done with Shen Te, you wicked person?

SHUI TA. I was her only friend!

ALL. Where is she?

SHUI TA. Gone away!

WANG. Where to?

SHUI TA. I'm not saying.

ALL. And why did she have to go?

SHUI TA (*yelling*). Because if she hadn't, you would have torn her to pieces.

A sudden silence descends.

SHUI TA (*has collapsed back on to his chair*). I can't go on. I want to explain everything. If everyone leaves except the judges, I will make a confession.

ALL. A confession! He's guilty!

FIRST GOD (*beats the gavel on the table*). Clear the courtroom!

THE POLICEMAN *clears the court.*

MRS SHIN (*smiling as she goes out*). This is going to be a surprise!

SHUI TA. Have they gone? Every one? I can no longer be silent. I recognised you, O Enlightened Ones!

SECOND GOD. What have you done with our good person of Sichuan?

SHUI TA. Let me confess the terrible truth to you: I am your good person!

He takes off his mask, and rips off his clothes, SHEN TE *stands revealed.*

FIRST GOD. Shen Te!

SHEN TE. Yes, it's me, I am Shui Ta and Shen Te.

> Your instruction once given me
> To be good and to live
> Ripped me in two like a lightning bolt.
> I don't know how it came about: I could not be
> Good to others and at the same time to myself,
> To help others and myself was beyond me.
> Oh, your world is so difficult!
> Too much hardship, too much despair.
> Hold out a hand to help,
> And it will be torn off! Aid the straggler,
> And you yourself are lost! Who could long refrain
> From becoming evil, where dog eats dog?
> From where was I to draw all that was needed?
> Only out of myself! But that finished me off!
> The weight of good intentions
> Crushed me. But when I did ill,
> Then I went around in pomp, and ate the best meat.
> Something must be wrong with your world.
> And why is there a reward for wrongdoing,
> And why do such harsh punishments
> Await the good? Oh, I felt such a desire
> To spoil myself! And there was a secret
> Wisdom in me, because my foster-mother
> Washed me in gutter water. That
> Sharpened my eye. But pity
> So hurt me, that I fell into a savage temper
> At the sight of misery. Then
> I felt myself changing, and
> My lips becoming hard. The kind word
> Tasted as ashes in my mouth. And yet
> I wanted to be an angel in the suburbs.
> To give was bliss to me. A happy face,
> And I walked on air.
> Condemn me: all I did
> I did to help my neighbour.
> To love the man I loved, and
> To save my little son from poverty.
> For your great plan, O gods,
> I was human and too small.

FIRST GOD (*with every sign of outrage*). Speak no further, unhappy woman! What are we to think, who were so overjoyed to find you again!

SHEN TE. But you must understand that I am the bad person whose misdeeds have been decried by everyone!

FIRST GOD. The good person of whose goodness all have spoken so warmly.

SHEN TE. No, the bad one too!

FIRST GOD. A misunderstanding! A few unfortunate incidents. Excess of zeal!

SECOND GOD. But how is she to go on living?

FIRST GOD. She'll manage. She's a strong, well-built person, who can take a lot.

SECOND GOD. Did you not hear what she said?

FIRST GOD. Muddled, very muddled stuff: incredible, highly incredible. Are we to admit that our commandments are fatal? Are we to scrap our commandments? (*Determinedly.*) Never. Is the world to be changed? How? By whom? No, everything is all right!

He quickly brings down his gavel on the table.

And now (*At a sign from him, music tones, a rosy light appears.*)
It is time to return. This little world
Was fascinating. Its joys and sorrows
Have enchanted and pained us. However,
Let us go on thinking beyond the stars
Of you, Shen Te, the good person, with pleasure,
Manifesting our spirit down below,
Carrying our torch in the cold and gloom.
Farewell, tara!

At a sign from him, the ceiling opens. A pink cloud descends. Upon it, the gods very slowly rise up.

SHEN TE. O Enlightened Ones, don't! Don't go away! Don't leave me! What shall I do about Wang, who believed in me, and the homeless poor? And how can I defend myself against the barber whom I don't love, and Sun, whom I do? And I'm

pregnant, my son will soon be here, and be wanting to eat?
I can't stay here!

*She looks fearfully towards the door, through which her tormentors
will enter.*

FIRST GOD. You can do it! Just be good, and everything will
turn out fine!

*Enter the witnesses. They are astounded to see the gods hovering on
their pink cloud.*

WANG. Show your piety! The gods have appeared among us!
Three of the highest gods came to Sichuan to look for a good
person, and they found one, but . . . !

FIRST GOD. No buts! Here she is!

ALL. Shen Te!

FIRST GOD. She has not perished, she was only hidden. She will
remain in your midst, a good person!

SHEN TE. But I need my cousin!

FIRST GOD. Not too often!

SHEN TE. At least once a week!

FIRST GOD. No more than once a month!

SHEN TE. Oh, don't leave, Enlightened Ones! I haven't told you
everything. I need you so badly!

THE GODS *sing the* Trio of the Vanishing Gods on the Cloud

Really now we must be going,
It's high time that we weren't here.
Put through tests more thoroughgoing,
Our precious find might disappear.

Human bodies cast long shadows,
Blotting out the golden light.
Therefore now you must allow us
Home to our celestial heights.

Our quest has proved conclusively . . .
So let us speedily begone.
May praise ring out effusively

To the good person of Sichuan!

SHEN TE. Help!

While SHEN TE *desperately holds out her arms towards them, they disappear upwards, waving and smiling.*